Come to me, all you who are weary and burdened,
and I will give you rest.

Matthew 11:28

Ordinary
PEOPLE
FINDING
Jesus

An ordinary woman's journey to faith

PAULINE   HOWELL

Published by Zaccmedia
www.zaccmedia.com
info@zaccmedia.com

Published November 2015

ISBN: 978-1-909824-92-8

British Library Cataloguing-in-Publication Data
A catalogue record for this book is available from the British Library.

Zaccmedia aims to produce books that will help to extend and build up the Kingdom of God. We do not necessarily agree with every view expressed by the authors, or with every interpretation of Scripture expressed. We expect readers to make their own judgment in the light of their understanding of God's Word and in an attitude of Christian love and fellowship.

Acknowledgements

To my wonderful family and friends. I am so blessed to have you all in my life. All handpicked for me by Jesus. Thank you all for loving me the way you do. For your patience, kindness, love, care, consideration, constant prayers, support – just for everything. I would be lost without you all.

To my publisher, Paul Stanier. Thank you so much for your patience and kindness in helping me so much. You have been incredible and I am so grateful about how I was led to you for you to publish my book.

I needed a photograph of myself and was threatened by my family not to take a selfie but to get a professional photo taken. I went into Dumfries in Scotland to Beautiful Beginnings Photography. Amanda Strotter, thank you for my gift.

To Nick Morgan from Advanced Computer Support in Dumfries – a huge thank you for all your help in getting my book back from cyberspace. I did what only I could do and sent it off into space and couldn't get it back. Thank you.

To everyone else who has and will be working on the publishing of this book, thank you all so very much.

Finally, to *you* reading this. Thank you. Should you wish to contact me to chat about anything, ask anything, please do not hesitate. It would be my great honour to assist you in any way I can. Contact details at the end of the book.

PS: Kerrilee, Shawn, Jason and Justen. Please do not let me get to heaven and be alone there. Please give your lives to Jesus. Please do not leave this until it is too late. Life is short, don't waste it. I love you so much and want only good for you all.

Contents

Introduction

My life story is dedicated to the five most important people in my life. My beautiful daughter, Kerrilee, my son Shawn, my twin boys, Jason and Justen, and Jesus Christ, my Saviour.

I would also like to thank everyone for praying for me when I was at my lowest, for encouraging me, for emailing me, for messages; without you all, I would never have managed to finish my book when I did. I'm sure it would have taken years longer! There are just too many names to mention and I would be sure to forget some of you, but remember, Jesus has seen what you have all done for me and at the end of the day that is what actually counts. I have to make special mention of two incredible ladies, though: Ann and Tracey Bridger. Without these two ladies, I am not sure I would have ever finished the manuscript.

I am not highly educated. I am not a theologian. I don't even know my Bible as well as I should. What I am writing is my personal life story. Please bear in mind that this book has not been written to bad-mouth anyone. It is about my experiences, and my opinions. It is most certainly not my intention to try to hurt anybody, and I have changed some of the names in it to protect people's privacy and preserve their anonymity. But if I have hurt or offended any person through this book, then I ask you to forgive me. I am just an ordinary person, glorifying God with my life. I am what I am today because of Him and nothing else.

I want to tell you how I came to write my story. In May 2010 I was woken up from my sleep and felt the Lord telling me that I was going to write a book. I turned over and went back to sleep but was disturbed again and again, until I eventually sat up and said out loud, 'Well, I am not a writer!' and a quiet voice said, 'You just have to type and I will tell you what to say.'

I argued this for a few weeks, but the urge to write was so strong I eventually said, 'OK, Lord, I will type.'

That night I was again woken from my sleep, and I knew what the book was going to be called. Well… I *thought* I knew: FINDING JESUS. But the word 'ordinary' kept coming up. Over and over I kept hearing and reading about ORDINARY PEOPLE and then I clicked: 'Oh, Lord, the blonde has it now!' Thus this title.

I now started thinking that maybe this really was God talking to me.

A gentleman from my church had died, and I was asked to make a plate of food for the guests who were gathering after the funeral. I felt such an urge to go to the service, and I kept asking myself if I had gone completely crazy; I never even knew the man. The urge was so great I went in and sat right at the very back. The moment the minister, John Koning, started speaking about Matthew 11:28, I knew without a doubt that this was why I was sent to a stranger's funeral service. This was the verse that God wanted on the cover of my book.

I want you to know it is not by chance that you are reading this; Jesus is calling you. When you get to the end of the story, you will have *no* doubt in your mind that we have a good, loving God. God is your heavenly Father, and wants you to be His child. He sent His Son, Jesus, to make a way for us to be right with Him. He did this when He died on the cross, taking the punishment we deserve for everything we have said and done to hurt God and others. And then Jesus rose from the dead, to prove that everything He said was true. If Jesus can keep loving a sinner like me, then how much more will He love you? He loves me unconditionally. He will love you just the same.

I have been asked what makes my life special or any different to the next person's. The only answer I have is that it is absolutely no different or special to your story. You may have had or are having an even harder walk in life than I did, but this is my story. This is me, an ordinary person, trying to give you *hope*.

This is my life.

Pauline Howell
Summer 2015

1

In the Beginning

I was born on 24 October 1963 to Ronald James Howell, British born, and Priscilla Mary Hunt, South African born. I was girl number three. The hospital was the Mater Dei Private Hospital, which today is the maternity section of the Frere Hospital in East London, South Africa. Then, on 21 November 1963, my father – a cabinet maker who had only just ventured out on his own – died from a very serious cholesterol problem.

I can only imagine how my poor mother must have suffered. She was left with no money, two little girls and a three-week-old baby. Life must have been extremely tough. My mother never said too much about this time in her life, except how wonderful my dad was – and how she had so wished I was a boy.

I have no early memories. I find this strange, as I talk to so many people who can remember right back to about two years old. My daughter is one of these people. My first memory is of a Christmas party and I was given a red pram. How old was I? I have no idea. I remember my sisters and I spent the entire night eating ice cream cones as fast as we could. We didn't get ice cream often, and I think we tried to make up for a lifetime in one evening. I remember we vomited all night. I wonder if we even cared, as we had enjoyed scoffing ice cream so much. The next day I remember taking my 'babies' out in my beautiful red pram. I was tall, as I had to bend over to push it. This is the only memory I have, and as I say, I have no idea what my age was.

My mother had met a man. His name was Brian Alstrom, but people called him Kimo. Kimo had a serious drinking problem and was definitely schizophrenic. I think my mother knew this before she married him, though I may be wrong. I think when someone is on their own with three little girls and life is a constant battle, they may sometimes settle for less than they deserve – maybe out of fear. Or maybe they don't think they could ever do better than what they have found.

What can I say about life with Kimo? When he was sober I truly loved him. He seemed such a kind, loving, gentle man, but when he started drinking brandy and coke, he turned into a monster. Life became hell.

My mother had, after many, many miscarriages, eventually managed to have her son. Her little boy at last! He was born on the 5 May 1973 and was the apple of my mother's eye: Brendon Harold Alstrom.

All I really remember is running, running, running. At all times of the night we would have to be ready to run as the voices in Kimo's head told him to kill us. He would be after us with a knife or a gun or his fists, or whatever else he managed to get hold of. Two o'clock, three o'clock in the morning would see my sisters, myself, my tiny brother and my mother on the run anywhere that was safe for us to hide away. I had a severely swollen, almost broken nose from being punched while trying to help my mother get away from his fists. The police were constantly been called to our house. Life was very tough. I don't remember us as a family ever discussing the way it was. We all seemed to just accept that this was a way of life.

Kimo loved to go fishing. He was also a brilliant carpenter. I remember walking into the garage to find a wooden boat he was making, and thought how magnificent this was going to be when he finished it. But he never got to finish this truly beautiful wooden boat. We used to go fishing a lot, all over the place. I seem to remember the Transkei being his favourite place. I recall nights out, with fishing and heavy drinking. Once we were in one of his boats going down a river in the Transkei when an unexpected wave overturned our boat. I could not swim, and I remember Kimo rushing to save me. Brendon, who was ten years my junior, was left to my mother to help.

I don't remember much of Brendon as a baby; my life was so absorbed in survival. After Brendon was born, Kimo had to go to Queenstown, to Komani, to an institution for people with mental issues. All I really remember about this place was that it was very, very cold. My mother had an old green two-toned car, and we used to pack blankets and sandwiches for our day trips to Queenstown so that my mother could spend time with Kimo. My sisters and baby brother and myself would stay in the car while my mother went into the big ominous-looking building for hours and hours. When we became bored, we would walk around the streets. We found a strange, round reddish fruit hanging over people's fences. After one taste I was hooked on pomegranates for life.

On the trips back home in the late afternoons, my mother would tell us that Kimo was undergoing very good treatment and when he got home everything was going to be wonderful. That was the first time I heard about electroshock treatment (electroconvulsive therapy – ECT). When I asked my mother what this was, she said they attached things to Kimo's head that would then send electricity to his brain which shocked him, and this would heal all his problems. He wouldn't drink anymore and the voices in his head would die so he wouldn't want to hurt us anymore.

I don't think Kimo stayed in Queenstown for a long time (maybe a month or two), but I recall the day he came home. When we walked into our house, he looked at my mother and said that there had better be an 'effing' bottle waiting for him. I was under the impression that he had been cured of alcohol addiction, but this was sadly not the case. A bigger monster had come home.

Over time we developed a strategy which seemed to work fine – for a while, at any rate. When he started punching my mother, I would grab the baby, and my sister Colleen his bottles with milk. My other sister, Leslie, had the big task of getting my mother away from Kimo. Leslie would taunt him, or swear at him, or throw something at him. She would then turn and run and he would give chase, leaving my mother. Colleen would quickly help my mother up, and we would take off in the opposite direction. Kimo's attacks could happen at any time; one night my mother only had her panties and bra on, and we were running down the back of the house through

Devil's thorns, though the fear was so great that he would catch us, we never felt them until much later. Our feet would throb and ache for hours.

I had the job of making the baby keep quiet, and though he was under one year old I swear he understood that he had to not make a sound. This particular night we didn't want Kimo to know that we had run down the garden into the neighbour's yard. He was a British man and never once turned us away. My sister ran up to the elderly man's house to borrow a gown for my mother. I think he was used to us disturbing him at all hours of the night for help to hide us. One of these terrible nights, Colleen in her panic forgot the baby's bottle. I never want to relive that night. The tiny, innocent baby crying for his bottle and all of us trying to keep him quiet... We could hear Kimo outside, ranting and raving. The poor neighbour, to this day I am not sure how he put up with us. I don't remember seeing Leslie again until we went back home the next day. She would always just reappear, or so it seemed.

I had no friends at all. I was too scared to make friends, in case they asked to come home with me. How would I ever be able to keep the dark secret of what was happening in my home?

Every Sunday night in our house we ate fish, chips and salad. For some unknown reason, Sundays always seemed to be the worst of the week's nights. One particular Sunday night is still clear in my mind, even after all these years.

My mother had put Brendon to bed, and Colleen and I had finished supper and had gone to the bedroom we shared. Colleen was always fighting with me about still wetting my bed. We never had a television and would listen to the radio for hours – a big deal in those days, I must add. I heard a plate smash and knew it was 'run time'.

I bolted straight to my mother's room for Brendon, and have no idea what Colleen went to do. I ran up the passage and saw Kimo standing with his back to me, punching my mother repeatedly in the face. Leslie ran up to him and suddenly everything went quiet. He dropped my mother and turned around, staggered a bit, then looked down at her; she was battling to stand up. In a quiet voice he said: 'Your effing daughter just stuck me with a knife.'

He started walking towards me. I backed away, towards the front door. He came up to me, and my mother ran and pulled the knife out his back. It looked as though the knife was below his shoulder. Leslie and Colleen had disappeared, or if they were there, I only recall what my eyes were seeing... He lay down on the floor in front of me, whilst I was still holding my little brother, his baby son, and he told me he was cold, very cold. My mother told me to run and get him a blanket, which I did (my mother used that same rug for many years and it freaked me out), then I ran back and covered him. My mother was on the phone, ringing my uncle John, and the doctor. I stood watching Kimo. I watched as he battled to breathe. I watched him turn a greyish colour. I watched the fish and salad start to come out of his nose and yet I couldn't stop watching. He kept telling me he was cold. He then closed his eyes and I knew he was dead. May God forgive me but I was glad.

The police were called so often to our home to help us that my sister, Leslie, was tried and found to be not guilty of murder. She had taken away the hell for all of us, or so it felt.

I used to secretly thank her for saving us. My sister was now my hero. But I woke up for many years sweating and battling to breathe, lying in a wet bed, even though the nightmare was over.

Life got better. My mother received his pension monies. For the first time in my life I got some brand-new clothes, no hand-me-downs this time. I had always had to make sure, if I was wearing trousers, that my legs stayed close together, as by the time the trousers reached me there often wasn't any material left between the legs at the top; it was completely worn away.

Wow! I felt so pretty; new clothes. My mother built a swimming pool for us and bought us a television. It was around this time that Leslie got married. Colleen and I would rush home from school, do our homework and race to the lounge at around four in the afternoon and sit and watch the test pattern on the television until six o'clock when the programmes started. It was so funny. We would run as fast as we could to the toilet and fly back in case we missed something changing on the test pattern. Yes, life was better... much, much better!

2

Life After Kimo

Now I could start thinking of making friends. This, though, sadly, proved to be a problem. Most of my friends had fathers, and the more time I spent with them the more I yearned for one. What did I ever do to be punished by not having a father? I would watch my friends with their fathers and anger and resentment started to set in. If they had problems, Daddy would just sort them out for them. Later, I decided I needed a father – or a boyfriend.

I started going to church with my mother. She was a member of the Anglican Church and had always attended St Marks in Cambridge, a suburb of East London, South Africa. She told me I was christened in this church, and she had got married there to my father. So I decided to go. I even decided to be confirmed. The only thing I remember about my confirmation was that the other children would laugh at me behind my back because I dressed differently to them. After all this I realized that church and maybe even God was actually not for me. This was not what I needed in my life.

My sister Colleen was stunningly beautiful. She had long strawberry-blonde hair, and when she walked into a room nobody saw anyone except her. She used to have boyfriends that would come to take her out. I was very close to her, and Brendon, and I hated to be at home without her, so I used to beg to go with her. Today I realize how pathetic I was, begging to go on dates with my sister. Believe it or not, on occasions she would let me tag along. This, I believe, was when she didn't really like the guy. Her guy friends used to bring lots of chocolates, which the entire family enjoyed. When the doorbell rang, I used to get excited to see which guy was there and what he had in his hands. Colleen used to get mad with me, and I just used to laugh at her anger.

My mother bought Colleen a maroon Volkswagen that we had much fun in. Colleen was six years older than me, and she would plaster my face with make-up, make me hold a cigarette and off to the drive-in we would go. I would flash the cigarette and act like a grown woman and we would breeze into over-eighteens' movies. We really had fun together. This is probably where I got the taste for cigarette smoking; I started smoking heavily by the age of about twelve or thirteen.

I discovered Mills & Boon books at the age of about fourteen. This was a world I wanted to be part of. A beautiful world where everything always ended in beautiful romance. I joined the Cambridge library and in no time I think I had read every book they had in the Mills & Boon section. I also made one very special friend, Gee. She lived on a farm and with her around, life was always good. I spent time on her farm during the weekends, and she spent Monday to Friday at my house. I never had to feel embarrassed about our home or anything that happened in it. She always just seemed to understand, without saying a word.

Across the road lived twin boys, who I also spent much time with. In particular, Michael, Gee and I were very close and had so much fun together doing all sorts of crazy things. We would take the British neighbour's vegetables out of his garden and go and sell them back to him. I'm sure he knew exactly what we were up to. Or we would pick guavas that we knew were riddled with worms and go around Cambridge selling them. As soon as we had some money, we would run up to the corner café and buy sweets. During school holidays we would go on hikes and grumble bitterly on the walk back to my mother's house as to who had planned this long hike! It wouldn't be long and we would be on another venture together.

I went to Cambrige Preparatory, then onto Cambridge Junior, then Cambridge High School. At the end of each term we would have what was called a 'Civvies Day' but we had to pay R2.00 to go. My mother never used to have spare money, and Colleen always used to pay for me. She would also always buy me a special lunch for that day – chips, a coke and a chocolate. Secretly, I hated these days, as I was always looked down on for the clothes I wore. Even though I had new clothes, they were not fashionable at all. They were just practical clothing. I remember thinking, 'I am going to go to school and hold my head up and it will be over soon enough.' I did have a nice circle of friends in high school, but I have often wondered if we weren't the outcasts and that was why we clung together. The popular girls wanted nothing to do with us.

Sadly my mother had turned to alcohol when I was about sixteen. Maybe this was her way of forgetting all the ugliness. I clearly remember one evening she had been very upset by my sister and climbed on a chair to get a suitcase down from the top of the wardrobe. I asked her what was going on. She said she had had enough and was leaving. I hung onto her for hours, crying and begging her not to leave me. Eventually the problem was sorted out. Then Colleen moved out of the house. I remember feeling so abandoned by her. My beautiful sister had being molested in that house years earlier by a close friend of my mother's, and she just wanted out.

I must also add that this house had a strange, cold, dark feel about it. Friends and family members claimed they had seen dark, scary images of a man. My mother's friend spent a night in Leslie's old room and was woken up with the blankets being lifted up and down, up and down. She said that an image of a man all in black was standing at the foot of the bed. She said she would never sleep there again. She wasn't the only one to experience this. One of my friends one day said to me that I lived in the Amityville Horror house.

After Colleen left, it was just Brendon and I. My beloved mother would get up in the morning and go to work, and as soon as she walked in the door would grab a glass on her way to her bedroom to pour her first drink. By early evening I only remember her as falling all over the place and slurring until she would eventually just put herself to bed. This was difficult not only for me, but also for my brother.

3

ASJ

I had never had a boyfriend. Then one day I walked up the road for my mother to buy bread and milk at the local shop and I saw a man; he took my breath away.

I kid you not. This was love. For the first time in my life I felt what it was like to be loved by a man. Well – more accurately, I discovered a deep love for a male figure. He never discovered the same love for me. He became the air I breathed, the food I ate, my whole world. He kept telling me to leave school, as we were getting married. Before I met ASJ all I had wanted to be was a teacher; I wanted to teach standard two and three children. I was doing well up to this stage, and had never skipped a day of school in my life.

In truth, I was a scared young lady – I was scared of everything, terrified of life in general, but this man had become my everything and I stopped caring about anything except him. I started bunking off school to stay home with him. He was working in the harbour, and did different shifts. I didn't care about anything except this man. What I didn't know was that he had many other women he was visiting. He was good-looking and did have a way with the ladies! We all wanted to be his slaves. My best friend, Gee, used to catch the bus with him into town in the school holidays, as she worked in a pie shop. They used to stand and have long kisses together. This devastated me when I found out. My best friend, the one person I trusted completely, had let me down. This affected our friendship in a huge way and it was never the same again. The betrayal was just too great. I never trusted any of my friends after this – and it came out over time how ASJ was sleeping with most of my friends.

I was a virgin and he had never slept with a virgin, so unbeknown to me this gave me a massive advantage over the other girls. He was not prepared to give any of them up, but he felt he had to marry me as he had his own untouched, besotted idiot to control in any way it pleased him. I then started finding out about the other women, and life turned into hell all over again.

Here I was, a now seventeen-year-old girl besotted with the love of her life, only to discover he did not feel the same way. I tried to commit suicide a few times. I felt my life was over. Sadly, he was still the air I breathed, the food I ate, my whole world. He kept pushing me to leave school, and I have often wondered if it was fear that I might be more highly qualified than him, or if it was because he would have lost control of me if I stayed on. I left school and found a job with the South African railways and we moved into a scary flat in the rough Quigney area of East London. One Saturday lunchtime, on my way to visit my mother, I opened the front door and a man stood there with blood running down his head and face.

I screamed and slammed the door shut. This was the type of place I had chosen to live in.

I didn't really care, though, as I was with my love.

I did not know at this stage that ASJ smoked dagga (cannabis) very heavily. Then one night there was banging at the door and in stormed the police and started arresting him and me. I freaked out with fear. I didn't know what was going on. The police threw all our clothes and food all over the floor of our flat. I was crying hysterically. Then the police flung a dish (a big one at that) of dagga onto our bed; and they found dagga hidden amongst some of my clothes. ASJ said to them that I knew nothing about the dagga. I think one of them took pity on me and removed the handcuffs. They arrested ASJ and all left the flat. I eventually stopped crying and started running around, trying to find some of the women I worked with to help me. The one woman I bumped into on the street obviously felt sorry for this maniac running about crying all over the area. After I told her what had happened, she said the next day I must go to a lawyer in town and he would get ASJ out on bail. So the next morning found me at the lawyer's and then at the court building, sitting with strange people who scared me. ASJ came up some stairs through a hole in the floor. I found out later that the holding cells were under the court. He was let out on bail and eventually received a suspended sentence. I remember walking out of there so happy that I had him back. He promised me he would never again touch that stuff. If only he could have stopped his lies.

His parents lived about thirty kilometres from my mother's house. We would sometimes catch a train up there and walk to his uncle's so that he could smoke his dagga. We were walking one day in a forest area and I turned around and he had a gun pointed at my head. I asked him what he was doing and he just looked at me. He had stolen my mother's gun from her wardrobe and was planning on shooting me. Unbelievably, I loved him despite this. My mother was always telling me how things were going missing out of the house and garage but I refused to believe it could be him.

ASJ was a person who told incredible lies. The sad part was that he believed what he was saying. I believed what he was telling me until I started growing up. I think his life had scared him and he hid away in an unreal world.

One weekend he took me to Queenstown to an old lady who had raised him from a little boy. This woman told me she had been on a train when ASJ's mother sat down with him and opened the window and tried to throw him out. This old lady brought him up for many years until his mother went to fetch him again. From what I could put together, it seemed as though the mother had had an affair and the present husband did not want this little boy. On this particular weekend in Queenstown I battled with the icy cold weather while ASJ was chatting up someone else behind my back. He proposed to her. I discovered a letter she wrote to him, telling him the colour of the kitchen curtains of the home they would soon have. When I confronted him he said he couldn't help it if women ran after him all the time. What was wrong with me?! I told him the only way I would hang around was if we got married. He immediately agreed and we got married and life got worse.

I think I lived from day to day. I was just existing. The other women never went away, they just increased.

We got married on 11 August 1984 and I was so absorbed in ASJ and my misery that I don't even recall life around me. I don't remember my brother growing up or what was happening in my sisters' lives or what my mother was doing. It was all about me, me, me. Misery, misery, misery. Pain, pain, pain. Why did I stay in this relationship? I couldn't live without ASJ. People used to tell me how stupid I was, how weak I was, how pathetic I was; all I cared about was ASJ. I didn't care what people thought or said. He was my life, my air, my food.

4

Kerilee and Shawn

On 23 September 1985 I gave birth to the most beautiful, precious little baby girl. I named her Kerrilee and nobody was allowed to pick her up or breathe over her in case they gave her germs. When she was about three weeks old, I got very, very sick with milk fever. I had no idea what was happening to me. In those days, after you had had a baby and were a very young inexperienced mother, the clinic sometimes would call on you to make sure you were coping with your new baby. When the nurse arrived and saw the state I was in, she immediately knew how to treat me.

I have two very clear memories of incidents of that time in my life. When Kerri was two weeks old, I had to take her to the clinic. There sat one of my biggest hang-ups – a woman that ASJ just couldn't stay away from. She sat there and was trying so hard to see my precious little baby and there was no way I was letting that happen. That was one of the few times that I felt I had an upper hand. I had ASJ's baby.

The second incident was dressing Kerri up for a baby competition and walking up to town with her in her pram.

I was very angry that she didn't win the competition because there were no other babies more beautiful than her, or so I believed. I used to walk around the Quigney all day with her hidden in her pram. She was my little princess. Family members still tease me about how I had refused to allow them to look at her in her cot as I was scared of germs. I remember the first three months of her life; I used to sleep with my finger under her nose to make sure she was breathing.

At three months I went back to work. I used to sit and cry all day at having to leave Kerri. I battled for a long time to come to terms with this. I wasn't back at work very long when ASJ was transferred to Richards Bay. This was a very difficult time for me. He was free to do as he pleased. Kerri and I went to visit him for two weeks just before she turned one year old. I remember walking miles from the suburb where we were staying to the shopping centre to go and look around. Richards Bay seemed like a nice place for a holiday, but I wasn't sure about living there.

ASJ and I had been apart for many months when I was sitting at work one day and a man popped up in front of me. His name was Andre. I couldn't stop thinking of him. He was divorced and would never have considered having an affair with me, even though I was considering it. Before anything could happen between us, my transfer came through and Kerri and I left East London for Richards Bay.

I hated it there. The home phone used to ring all day and all night but nobody ever spoke. I wanted to get divorced and go back to Andre. But even though I wanted to be with Andre, I didn't know if I could live without ASJ.

Kerri was growing more beautiful by the day. She was such a tomboy, zooming all over the flat complex on her black scooter. She used to pop into all the neighbours' for a quick visit. One neighbour would give her a Vienna sausage, the next a piece of cheese, and so on. She was a massive hit with everyone. The neighbours loved her.

Kerri adored her father. All she wanted was to be with him. She was a proper little Daddy's Girl, and if he was around she would have nothing to do with me. My poor little girl was under the same spell as I was.

I remember the one day receiving a call from the crèche she was in to say that they were sorry but she could not attend nursery dressed the way she was. I had no idea what they were talking about, as ASJ had taken her to school that morning. I arrived at the crèche to find my little girl had put make-up on before going to school. My child's eyes and face where completely blue with eyeshadow. She really did look a sight. Well, all I did was laugh and laugh at the sight of her, took her home and washed her face clean. When I asked her why she had done that, she said she wanted to look like me. How on earth could I be cross with her for wanting to wear make-up to school? I decided to try this affair thing. I hated it, but tried it again. If ASJ enjoyed it so much surely it had to be good?

My doctor in Richards Bay discovered I had cervical dysplasia. This is the stage before cancer. ASJ had to take me to Parklands Hospital in Durban for very intense laser treatment. This was very uncomfortable and all I remember was smelling burnt meat in the room. The doctor said that I should consider another child, as I may have to have a hysterectomy sooner rather than later. One year later, on 26 January 1989, my beloved little Shawn was born. I had spent most of this pregnancy on my own with Kerri. ASJ was supposedly working very long hours. I had gained a massive amount of weight with Shawn because all I remember eating was cheese. Cheese for breakfast, cheese for lunch, cheese for snacks and cheese for supper.

Almost two weeks after Shawn was born, ASJ arrived home early and I was complaining that the baby still had not been named. He said that he would be named Shawn because I had named Kerri. I never knew at that time that a girlfriend had in fact named him. He was such an amazing little baby. Beautiful and fat. Perfect.

I hadn't been out of hospital with Shawn for very long when I discovered ASJ's office keys at home, and hid them. Later that night I drove to his office with Kerri and the new baby and the security people let us in. In his office I found a diary from one of his girlfriends. In it she had kept an account of things they did together. Once again I was devastated. Once again I did nothing. I decided *no more children*. I was still thinking of moving back to Andre.

A month after Shawn was born I had a nervous breakdown. I think this was related to postnatal depression and trying to deal with all the stress and worry going on in my life. I was not coping at all and my doctor sent me to Durban, back to Parklands for treatment. I was in a ward with all the drug addicts and was trying to work out why on earth I was with these particular people. I was, after all, not a drug addict. It was only much later that I realized we all had a similar problem. Dependency on something.

My sister Colleen came to stay to help me with Kerri and this tiny new baby. Shawn never cried. It was almost as though he sensed trouble and just lay quietly in his carrycot all the time. Colleen commented to me that it was so strange that this little baby hardly ever cried. When I eventually got home from the hospital, I woke up the first night to see ASJ quietly leaving our bed completely naked and climbing into my sister's bed in the spare room opposite our bedroom. I think I died that night.

The next day my sister packed and ASJ drove her to Durban to fly back to East London. He waited in Durban because my mother arrived later that day. Colleen and I never spoke about what had happened.

My mother didn't stay long. We walked around the complex a lot, discussing what I should do. I was thinking of a private investigator, but as my mother eventually made me see, this would not help. I knew what was happening; the only thing I did not know was who the women were at the time. It was killing me. We decided for the children's sake it was time to stop thinking of me and start thinking of the children's lives.

This was probably the biggest decision I had made to date. I started to pack. I'd had enough of this life. But things were going to get worse.

When ASJ came home and saw me packing, he promised it would all end. He gave his word he would now seek help and change. Fool that I was, I again believed his lies.

5

The Twins

Shawn was three months old when I started having severe stomach cramps and eventually had to go to my doctor.

He did an ultrasound and, lo and behold, there were two tiny little heartbeats. I went mad. I cried and ranted and raved all the way home. How could this have happened? I was using a contraceptive! Why was I being punished like this? I couldn't even cope with Kerri and Shawn, and now two more! What was I going to do?

I locked myself, Kerri and Shawn in the bedroom that night and ASJ broke the door down in anger to slap me about a little. I was pregnant with twins, had two small children, and my life was a total mess. I had absolutely nobody I could turn to for help.

We got kicked out of the duplex we were living in because he was spending all the money on his pleasures and nothing was being paid. The sad part was that I didn't even know this was happening until the owner arrived at my door and said we had a week to move. Another shock.

It was around this time that I discovered a book on witchcraft. It looked as though ASJ was practising it. When I eventually confronted him he laughed in my face, and said the most difficult thing he had to find was the bat. Killing lizards and cats and all sorts of things… That was the day I realized what an evil man I was married to. Who exactly was he trying his witchcraft out on? This I will never know.

Working on the railways, I was able to get a place on what was called the Rank in Empangeni. This was a really scary area, almost in the middle of the sugarcane fields. The house I found was right at the very top of the fields, but at least it was a home for my children and me. By this stage I didn't see much of ASJ. He was around very little. I was pregnant with the twins and working and trying to take care of my little Kerri and Shawn.

I had a domestic worker helping me at home, as I had gone back to work. The children attended a crèche in Richards Bay. Some days they stayed with the domestic, as we never saw ASJ for days at a time. One day I got home to find the domestic worker missing. I walked all around the area asking neighbours what had happened to her. Eventually I found out that a man had approached her and asked for the key to my house. She said she couldn't do that because of the babies living in the house. He chopped off her hand that was holding the back door key with a *panga* (machete). He took her hand and left. She managed to make her way to the hospital. When I found out where she was, I rushed off to the hospital to find her, leaving the children with a neighbour I hardly knew. The domestic was lying in bed after the doctors had operated on her and done the best they could for her. She was crying, I was crying, and she told me not to stay in that house anymore. She told me to run away, to take my babies and hide, as the man who had hurt her was coming back to get us.

I was terrified and kept trying to contact ASJ at work but was told he had not been seen for a few days. I found out later that he had been caught again for dagga possession, but had turned pimp for the police, meaning that he would report other drug users and dealers to stay out of jail. I had no way of contacting him at all.

I raced home and collected my babies from the neighbour, and ran around the house locking windows and doors and pushing furniture up against the front and back doors. I took a screwdriver and pushed it into the lock of the back door. I banged the screwdriver in at an angle so that if the stranger tried he wouldn't be able to unlock the door. The only form of protection I had was a bread knife and this is what I walked around the whole night with in my hand.

At around two o clock that morning I heard him. He was there, trying to open the door. I was so scared, so terrified, words could never explain the fear I felt. All I did was scream and shout that I had a gun and I would shoot if he didn't go away. Eventually there was just quiet outside.

I was just over four months' pregnant at this time. A day later my amniotic sac ruptured.

I was pregnant with twins, and smoking heavily. I was rushed by ambulance from Richards Bay to Durban to St Augustine's Hospital. I immediately saw a gynaecologist who told me he didn't believe the odds of the babies' survival to be very high. He felt I would abort in a day or two.

I remember lying all alone in my ward thinking about what I was going to do. I didn't really want these babies, so why wasn't I feeling happy? But then it hit me. These were *my* babies. My gift! I decided to fight for them.

I wasn't religious but was planning on a prayer when an elderly gent walked into my room and asked if he could pray for me. I told him what had happened, and he started to pray. He asked Jesus to place one of His hands upon my tummy and hold these tiny babies in my womb, even though they were threatening to fall out.

'Hold them in, Jesus,' I also prayed.

I had to lie in hospital for just over a month. I was so worried about what was going on at home with ASJ, who had now been located, and my two children. I felt desperate to get back home. My amniotic sac had resealed and the water had refilled so the doctor felt I could go back home.

The fluid that is in the amniotic sac contains a mild antiseptic, thus protecting all babies from germs. I had been warned that the odds of infection setting in after ruptured waters was very high, and so I had to go for blood tests every day after I left the hospital. The way I remember the doctor explaining it to me was that there was a normal white blood cell count, and if it went up, reaching a certain figure, we would have to start considering an abortion, as the babies' brains would become affected. Every day the count grew higher and higher because of infection, until the gynaecologist told me they would have to abort the babies, as their little brains would now be badly affected.

Well, I went home and kept thinking of the little tract that the elderly gent had left with me in the hospital that day.

It said that we are like a garden and Jesus is like a gardener; he takes all the dead leaves and weeds out of the garden. The more I thought of this, I realized that these babies were definitely not weeds. I fell on my knees and asked Jesus again to please rest His hand on my tummy and take the infection out.

I couldn't believe what happened. The following day I again went in and they had drew blood to test. This was D-Day! Later that day I received a phone call and was told I no longer had to come in daily because the infection was *gone*! Completely gone!

Now I really started to think about this Jesus!

I hadn't been eating very well because there wasn't much money at this stage for food. I remember thinking that the food I ate that day, Kerri and Shawn could have eaten the next day. Yes, I was worried about my unborn babies, but without ASJ around – he had gone again – I couldn't even get to a shop.

I remember having an appointment with the gynaecologist on a Thursday and walking into his consulting room. He looked at me and told me that I could actually go home because whoever was looking after me and my unborn babies, nobody medically could do more. He also said that I needed to try to keep the babies in for at least another month for them to survive in a Durban hospital. Three days later, Sunday morning, I woke to feel water running down my legs in the bed. My sac had ruptured for the second time. Luckily ASJ had been home and I asked him to drive me to St Augustine's Hospital in Durban. He took Kerri and Shawn to friends in Richards Bay, and then took me to Durban. When I arrived at the hospital I was immediately examined. My Durban gynaecologist told me to try to hold the babies until at least the Tuesday. They then started cortisone injections – so much that I wasn't allowed any cortisone again until 1999. It was now 1990! The cortisone was to try to get their little lungs ready for breathing.

My mother phoned that afternoon and told me she had managed to book a flight to Durban the next day at around lunchtime. This was all happening on the Sunday and I couldn't think anymore. I was scared. I was alone. I was worried about Kerri and Shawn.

The following day, my mother walked in at about one o clock, and how I cried and cried with such relief. On that Monday, at 2.15 p.m., twin one was delivered naturally (even though the gynaecologist said this might not happen as twin two was breech), and then all contractions stopped. Medication was given to me immediately and at 2.23 twin two arrived. I had pushed with such strength he had turned and came into the world head first. Two identical little boys came out screaming; little boys who were not ready for this world. Premature babies, born on the 22 January 1990 without the aid of oxygen. Two little baby boys fighting for life. I now had three little boys all under the age of one… Shawn turned one year old four days later, on 26 January.

These twins wowed me from the minute I laid eyes on them. They were so tiny, so perfect, I couldn't even pick them up. They had to stay in high care at St Augustine's Hospital for a long time. My babies' weight was identical, the femur bones and the head circumference measured identically. They lay in one incubator side by side, two little babies with the same everything. I was up and down to high care staring at this strange sight, trying to absorb how I was ever going to be able to tell them apart. In order to know who was who, I had to look at the belly buttons. Was this clamp one or clamp two? That is how I referred to these identical little babies.

On day two, clamp two needed medication to help speed up the brain as he had forgotten to breathe. Apparently this is common in twins born prematurely. The staff at this hospital were unbelievable. They never looked me in the face; their eyes were constantly scanning these tiny babies lying all over the room in incubators, all premature. They were a team of highly trained sisters, no nurses. My little twin two was noticed as having stopped breathing instantly and all they did was flick him with a finger to remind him he had to breathe if he was going to live.

These tiny babies were fed through the nose with little tubes. I was pumping my milk out of my breasts which was tube-fed to my babies. On ASJ's one and only visit we had a fight because I was having a sterilization. No more babies for me. At first he refused to sign the document and threw it in the bin, and I remember screaming and making a scene until he felt so embarrassed he grabbed it out of the bin, signed it and walked out.

The following morning I had my operation. I remember waking up with pain I had never experienced before. It was so bad I started to deeply regret my decision to be sterilized.

One week later I went home, back to Richards Bay, without my babies. This was a terrible time emotionally for me. I felt so torn, as I wanted to be with Kerri and Shawn and I wanted to be with my new babies. With nobody to really share with, it really was a bad time for me.

The distance between Richards Bay and Durban is roughly about 177 kilometres. Every second day I would travel to Durban to be with my babies. Every other day I would express my breast milk and take it to the blood department and they would have the milk delivered to the hospital.

On one of these visits I walked into high care where they were still in their incubator and a nappy had been rolled up to part them. When I enquired why this had been done, the sisters laughed and said they kept pulling each other's tubes out their little noses. They seemed to be feisty little boys.

I still had not named these little boys and decided that as it seemed to me that Jesus had been looking after them from day one, I would call them something beginning with J, for Jesus' children. This is how Jason and Justen got their names.

When they turned six weeks old they were allowed to come home. What a happy, happy day. My babies were home. I wouldn't have to drive up and down on my own anymore. ASJ drove us; I remember fighting with him going back to Richards Bay as he wouldn't close the window, and the wind was so strong in the back of the car with the babies. It was always just about him.

It was probably a day or two after I got home that ASJ told me it would be best for me to leave town with the four children and go back to my mother in East London as it was all going to hit the fan and he didn't want us there when it happened. I cried and begged him to tell me what he had done. He just said, 'Go, and I promise I will come and fetch you and the children as soon as things blow over.'

He spent a last night with us and we never slept at all. I think I knew it was the last night I would have with him. We just lay and held each other. I recall begging ASJ not to leave us forever. He said that as soon as he had sorted out all his problems he was coming to fetch us. He promised me and I again believed him.

6

Leaving ASJ

Early the following morning I left Richards Bay for good. I travelled with Chris, Leslie's husband, who was driving my car with two of the children, and Colleen and her boyfriend in their car with the other two children. It was a long, very tearful trip from Richards Bay to East London. I couldn't stop crying and knew this was affecting my children, but just couldn't stop. Poor Chris had me crying for over ten hours and he never once complained. Driving through the Transkei should have been scary but I was just too wrapped up in my own pain. I remember thinking that life was over for me. I had no idea what was still to come. These are the only thoughts I remember on the drive back to East London. What the children did I cannot tell you; so self-centred back then, I only remember my pain.

My purse had exactly R5.00 in it when I arrived at my mother's house. Money that was due to me from the railway was still to be paid and could possibly take months.

My mother was wonderful to us. But I had to stay in Leslie's old room, the room I hated and feared, because Brendon had the only other big bedroom down the passage. For about two weeks I moped around crying a lot, waiting for ASJ to come and fetch us. I think I knew this was never going to happen, but I clung on to hope. I was battling with the four children. The twins woke up every three hours to feed, Shawn was a tiny one-year-old and my little Kerri was getting ready to start pre-school. I felt as though I was dead inside. Why did I have to suffer this way? I was barely coping with life. I was depressed, I was lonely, I was scared. I felt empty.

Colleen's boyfriend managed to get me a job on the fresh produce market in Wilsonia where he worked. I thought that I needed to try to start my life again. My starting pay was R80.00 per week. I was only working four hours a morning, but I felt the need to be around other adults. I slowly began to feel life return to me.

Around the corner from where my mother lived was a day crèche and I felt it would be good for Kerri to mix with other children. I sent Shawn with her. The lady who ran the crèche was very good to me, charging me a very low rate for the two children to attend mornings only. I would get a lift there at lunchtime from work and we would walk back to my mother's house. Jason and Justen stayed home with a domestic helper in the mornings while I was at work.

Working helped me to start finding myself. I also went to see a psychiatrist at the Frere Hospital, as I felt I really needed some medical help.

I was put into hospital for a few days just so they could monitor the medication they had started me on. The psychiatrist asked me to look back into my life and tell him what I saw, and the scary thing was that all I could see was black, black and more black. After I responded well to the medication I was sent home again. Between Colleen, my mother, the domestic help and myself, the children were well looked after. I started to look forward now. Life was a little easier.

Brendon had just got back from the navy on a pass and I was feeling happier than I think I'd felt in a long, long time. It was so good to spend time with him. My children where growing nicely. Kerri was due to start school in the January but I started to feel lonely. Brendon left again for the navy and all I did was work either on the market or on the four children. The work never seemed to stop. Bath Shawn, then twin one then twin two, then Kerri. Then hand-feed the three boys as they were too little to feed themselves. Change nappy after nappy, towel nappies in those days, which I soaked in sterilizing powder and then hand-washed. It never stopped. I was starting to hunger for after-hours adult company. My mother was never around in the evenings for long due to her drinking.

It must have been about ten months that I was back with my mother that I phoned Andre. I wondered why he hadn't contacted me. A lady answered the phone and I asked to speak to Andre and the phone went silent. After a few long seconds, another lady came on the phone and said she was very sorry to tell me but he had died in a motor vehicle accident on his way home from up-country. I was devastated.

I started drinking, and sneaking out of the house late at night. I would wait until the children were fast asleep, then I would slip out. I would hitchhike or walk down to drinking spots in the Quigney. I don't think I really cared about anything anymore except my children. I was so lonely, and couldn't see a future. Here I was, not thirty yet and with four children; what was I going to do with this screwed-up life?

Every single weekend, regardless of what the weather did, I took my children out somewhere. When I look back it amazes me how I did so much on so little money. We went to the zoo or the aquarium or we went to a place called Marina Glen that the children all loved. The twins were over a year old by now. At Marina Glen we would ride on the train, or the boats or the cars, all kiddies' rides available, or we would eat our picnic lunch on the grass and lie about and chat and laugh. My children and I were and are very, very close. I lived for these children. They had become my life. But the feelings in me were of longing.

Once a month I would take the children to the Cambridge cemetery to my father's grave. My father was buried three feet deeper than the normal depth of a grave, as my mother was supposed to be buried above him. So it was soil until my mother joined my dad. I never had any gardening tools so I used to take five of my mother's kitchen forks and off we would go to the grave. We would each be armed with a fork and would dig all the weeds out. The children loved this. I hate to think now what my poor mother would have said had she seen us digging with her kitchen forks!

I used to sit and talk to my dad. I felt so much anger towards him. I believed that if he had lived my life would have taken a different path. I would sit and moan at him, and at God. My children got so used to this conversation that I had going on every month with the soil that they didn't even blink anymore. I felt so angry that my father could have died on me. These visits went on for years.

Then, I met a chap who was visiting his sister down the road from my mother's house and was very attracted to him, but there seemed to be something about this man that I couldn't work out. I eventually felt he had probably just come out of prison, and when he next visited me I confronted him about my suspicions. He never once denied it, and told me he had been in prison for about ten years for murder.

We started to develop a friendship. He was lonely and I was lonely. Over a few months our friendship deepened and with this came smoking dagga with him, and drinking. This is what he did so I thought, 'OK, I'm not hurting anyone by smoking with him.' My children were at all times well looked after. I don't know if dagga did anything for me except to make me giggle and eat a lot. I tried to only ever smoke with him at night after the children were asleep.

This relationship lasted about five months. The wonderful thing about being with him was that he only had eyes for me. He made me feel like I was cherished and loved. He made me feel wonderful.

He had a motorcycle and we would often go down to the beach at night and walk and smoke and laugh, and I felt a sense of happiness.

Then I woke one morning and decided that I was actually over this. I was tired of the drinking, the dagga-smoking, the constant going out. Surely there must be more to life than this.

I was still sneaking out a lot. I was doing a lot of things that I am too ashamed to mention. I was still drinking and partying heavily. I remember just wandering around the Quigney late at night meeting complete strangers and going with them to smoke dagga. How nothing bad happened to me is a miracle.

The turning point came when one morning I got back to my mother's house at about 2 a.m. and all four of my children were lying awake, waiting for me. This broke me. Looking into their perfectly innocent faces I realized it was time to grow up and stop thinking about me all the time.

I stopped going out altogether. But the hunger for someone to love me deeply, honestly, genuinely, faithfully, truthfully, completely just never went away.

A couple of nights after my decision, I was lying in bed crying. I was reading the Bible, the book of Psalms, crying out to Jesus for help with my life. I eventually turned the light out and had not even turned over when something grabbed me by the shoulders and tried to pull me off the bed. My nails were long and beautiful and I snapped most of them off by trying to hang onto the bed. I eventually found my voice and started to say the Lord's Prayer, and a dead silence came over the room. I was absolutely terrified. My nails were broken and my fingertips were bleeding.

This never happened again. What it was I don't know, but it was very scary.

7

Brendon

Brendon was home from the navy for good now. He and I and his friends were spending lots of time together. I think what made Brendon and I close was my mother's drinking. We both hated it. When his buddies came over, my mother used to try to hang around them, but this embarrassed Brendon as his friends had to watch our mother slurring and falling about. He would always come and fetch me to take her away. I would usually tell her to come and look at something going on, on TV.

My mother had had a rondoval put into the backyard for Brendon to live in. I think it was too busy inside the house with all of us. My mother and my brother sacrificed a huge amount for my children and me to live with them. I realize today how great the sacrifice was. At the time I just took it for granted. My boys went through a phase of crayoning on the walls; I always painted over it and fixed it up but I don't think I was really very grateful for what my mother and brother had done for us.

I began going to church with my mother and the children. This was one thing I was very strict about – my children had to go to church. Maybe I was hoping they could make up for my sins. I started going with them, but that didn't last long. I overheard some members discussing how my mother was such a drunkard and why did she bother coming to church. This angered me very deeply as I felt no one other than the family had the right to talk about our mother's problems. They had no right to speak badly of her. They had no idea of the life she had led. Who did they think they were to point fingers at my mother? That was the end of me and church again.

Colleen and her boyfriend started going through a rough time. Colleen had started drinking very heavily by this stage. She and I hung around together quite a lot, and we became very close again. Then one evening I received a phone call from ASJ's girlfriend to tell me that they were getting married. My divorce had been finalized and he was moving on. I had gone through legal aid and they had provided me with a lawyer and I was told to appear in court and it was all over before I could blink an eye.

All those years spent together over in minutes! It felt wrong, somehow.

I was with my children constantly, and had stopped going out completely, when one night my friend Marie said she was taking me out to a movie. This was in September 1993.

We left all the children watching TV with the babysitter and left for the movies. When we arrived, the movie we wanted to see was already halfway through so we decided to go home. On the way to the car, Marie suggested we had a drink first. I was really against this as I was trying to turn my life around. She won, though I made her promise only *one* drink.

We sat down at the bar and ordered a drink. We chatted and laughed when I noticed a lady down the bar staring at me. I asked Marie if she knew who the lady was, and she said she didn't. Then I noticed the man sitting in front of her was watching me also. He suddenly got up and came over as he knew Marie and wanted to meet me. It then came out that the woman sitting with him was trying to chat him up and was angry that he was watching me. That was the start of John and me.

What can I say about John? He was funny, charming, entertaining, loving, generous, and he genuinely seemed to love my children. I came with 'baggage' – four beautiful children.

I fell in love with John very quickly. It seemed my time for favour had truly come. John and I went out every weekend, drinking and partying. Life was good. Some weekends I would take the children to their aunty Rose on ASJ's side of the family, and this they thoroughly enjoyed. They loved going to Aunty Rose. John would take me on his boat for the weekend. We would fish non-stop. I think this was when I was at my happiest. The only thing missing was my children.

I was still living with my mother, and John and I decided to get engaged. Things seemed to be moving quickly but I felt sure this was right. We planned our engagement for 31 December 1993, but this sadly never happened.

On the Thursday evening I'd been lying in my bed with the children watching TV when Brendon came in and said that he and his friend Brendon Bleach were going out for a while. I argued with him because he had to help me with so much the next day, with my big engagement only two days away. He told me to relax, he would be home early, and he left. I never saw my brother alive again.

The following morning, I went off to work as usual. Working on the market meant starting early, and I had left home before six in the morning.

Around seven o'clock, a lady came and informed me that there had been a death in my family. I suddenly couldn't breathe and immediately thought Shawn had died. Why I had this thought I cannot say. We starting walking down the market and I was by now sobbing uncontrollably and battling to breathe when I asked the woman if it was my Shawn. She very sadly shook her head and said it was my brother, Brendon.

Writing this now brings tears to my eyes. All the years I had managed to protect him, I had now failed him. In the blink of an eye, my baby brother was gone. He hadn't even turned twenty-one. Brendon and his friend had been at a disco when they decided they were going home. Paul Rusch, another friend, was taking his girlfriend home, so Brendon got in the back. His friend jumped into the front seat once the girlfriend had got out. When they were driving over the Batting Bridge on their way to Cambridge, the car started to skid as it had been raining quite a lot. At that time another man, who had just left the disco, also came screaming down the road in a Hummer-type vehicle and ploughed straight into the car. It sounded as though Brendon and his friend died instantly, though witnesses said that the driver was still trying to talk. All three boys were twenty years old, and had not had a drop of alcohol in their systems. Three families lives in turmoil. Three families' lives destroyed.

No goodbyes. No hugs. No 'I love you's. Nothing. Just gone. Final. Over.

I spent a very long time trying to imagine what Brendon had gone through. Was he scared? Did he know he was going to die? Did it hurt? I drove myself crazy with all these questions to which I eventually came to realize I would never find answers to.

After that day I basically watched my beloved mother try to drink herself to death. She gave up all will to live after that. I watched how the other families suffered. .

I couldn't get over Brendon's death. I felt so haunted. One night I woke up crying hysterically as I'd had a dream that was unbelievably real to me. Brendon woke me up and was holding me and clearly told me he was OK and that I must stop crying and let him go. After this I felt better.

Life carried on.

8

John and Me

John and I moved into Colleen's house around the corner from my mother, as my sister had met a new man and they had moved to Pietermaritzburg. He had a job on the market there. I was very involved with John and my children and working on the market and keeping house.

Then Colleen put the house that we had been renting on the market. We managed to get the deposit together and bought it. My first home! I worked like a man on my home; John at this stage had no interest in the house. He had a gambling addiction, an alcohol addiction and a nicotine addiction, but he was very good to my children and me. Without John, I would never have managed to have a home of my own. I loved it. I did all the painting that needed to be done, and I did most of the garden work. So between getting up at 2 a.m. in the morning, arriving at the market at 3 a.m. and working until 3 p.m. most days, I also spent time with my children, cooked, gardened, painted, did homework, packed lunch boxes, prepared breakfast for my children for the morning before I left for work, and watched either Kerri swimming or the boys playing rugby. I worked harder than most women I knew, but this was for my children.

In summer, weekends were a fun time for us. I love the beach and water and outdoors with a passion, so on Saturdays in summer I would pack a picnic basket and we would go to the beach for the entire day. Swim, tan, run around, build sandcastles... just have fun. Those are good memories. John was very rarely with us. He always said he had to work.

John wanted to get married. I said I would never marry again and wanted nothing to do with getting married. In August 1999 he took me to Oudtshoorn and I fell in love with this beautiful place and the beautiful people. Whilst driving around I mentioned that if I were to ever marry again it would be in this town.

In the December he told me he had made all the arrangements and the children and I were going to Oudtshoorn, where John and I were going to get married. My children had never really had a holiday up to this point; I was angry with him as I felt he was bribing me. How could I say no? Here was an opportunity for my children to have a holiday! So on 14 December 1999 we got married in a little Methodist church and it really was lovely. The organist who we didn't know ended up also witnessing our marriage. The church itself was beautiful, covered with ivy on the outside walls. We got married before God but sadly not in God.

Afterwards John took us to the Holiday Inn for supper, and I watched the joy on Shawn's face at being able to jump up and down and serve himself. He could pick and choose any food he wanted. I, on the other hand, ate nothing, but I drank so much champagne that I don't even remember going home.

It was around this time that I begged John to go to church with me. I had this huge problem about doing anything on my own where people would look at me.

I continued to insist my children go to church every Sunday. Around the corner from where we lived was a choice of two churches. They chose Cambridge Baptist as their church so this was where I decided John and I would try. We arrived on a Sunday morning at 9 a.m. for a Bible class. The teacher started his lesson and we had to move from one part of the Bible to another part. I nearly died; all these people could see that I had no clue what the Old Testament was to the New Testament. I had no clue how the Bible worked, and after a few Sundays I decided to avoid the embarrassment. Staying away from church seemed so much easier.

9

Finding Jesus

My beautiful, kind-hearted, generous and caring sister Colleen loved to read and would always be found with a book in her hand. I think she tried to do and hide herself in her books. She worked on the Municipality/council, right up into the supervisor's position. She had really done well for herself but my beautiful sister also had weaknesses that she could not handle. Colleen believed she had to have a man in her life and, as with me, I don't think she was very fussy. If he paid her attention and bought her some wine, she was in love.

Over the years I watched my sister's life fade away. She turned to alcohol, lost everything she had worked for, and ended up as a car guard in Pietermaritzburg. This not only saddened me but angered me so much. 'How could she have allowed a man to do this to her?' I thought. But who was I to point a finger? Her boyfriend at this time eventually drank himself to death and my sister Leslie went up to Pietersmaritzburg to fetch Colleen and bring her back to our mother in East London.

Colleen came home and things were strained between us. I walked into the house one afternoon and she was drinking heavily. I asked her where she was getting the alcohol from and what she said to me I am not able to repeat, but it angered me so much that I phoned Leslie and we tried to have Colleen admitted into hospital for the help she needed. According to her, however, she never had a drinking problem. She wouldn't speak to me after this. In fact, we never spoke to each other again because on 26 June 2000 all her organs shut down and she died alone in the Frere Hospital in East London.

I was absolutely devastated. How could she have done this to me? How could she have not told me how bad she felt inside? How could she have just left without so much as a goodbye? How dare she? She was forty-three years old and one of the most beautiful women I'd ever known. When she walked into a room her presence was just so powerful people did not see anyone else.

She died without giving me a chance to tell her how much I loved her and how deeply sorry I was, or before I could ask for her forgiveness. I never got the chance to explain that I only wanted to help her. I wanted her to have a long and happy life without alcohol. But she was gone. No second chances.

I could have done more. I should have done more. I was again wrapped up in myself, my life, and didn't push hard enough to help her.

She just left us. She also left a beautiful daughter and a beautiful son.

After Colleen died in 2000, I decided to try church again.

There was a woman called Barbara who lived across the road with her mother. She had recently lost her husband and was also wanting to go to church. So off to Cambridge Baptist Church we went. After a few times of attending on a Sunday night, the pastor, Bruce Davie, asked if anyone wanted to 'give their lives to Jesus'. I had such a strong urge to get up out of my seat, but was too scared to do it on my own. I didn't have the courage to stand up in front of all those people. On the way home I asked Barbara if she would get up with me next time they gave that call to stand up. The next Sunday we stood up together and gave our lives to Jesus. We had heard about what He had done for us on the cross, that He had paid the price for all our sin, all our offences against God and other people, and that He rose from the dead and is alive today; and that He sent His Holy Spirit to people who want to follow Him, to give them power to live for Him, and to have changed lives.

Did fireworks go off, did happiness explode, did wonderful things happen? No. This did not happen for me. I felt the same, I acted the same. It felt as though nothing had happened. I still smoked fifty-plus cigarettes a day. I still drank. I still partied. I was still the same… or was I?

I started going to church every Sunday night, and I slowly started to read my Bible. I learnt through Cambridge Baptist Church that God is in fact also Jesus and also the Holy Spirit. I thought, 'How on earth can this be possible?' I started going to a grown-up type of Sunday school offered by the church and led by a man called Mike Kruger. I respect this man so much as he taught me most of what I know about Jesus today. I began learning all about my Bible, about

God, about Jesus, about the Holy Spirit. I never saw any change in myself at all – I don't think I was looking – until one day my daughter said to me, 'You know, you always used to shout and scream at us, and you don't do that so much anymore.'

Wow, what a slap in the face that was! The fruits of the Spirit – 'love, joy, peace, forbearance, kindness, goodness, faithfulness, gentleness and self-control' (Galatians 5:22-23) – had been working in me all this time and I had believed that nothing had changed! What God was this that He loved me after all that I had done? I had been to hell and back. I had done bad, bad things and yet He kept saying to me, 'Come to me, because I love you.' This was a big deal for me. I battled with this. I slowly started to give a little more of me to this God who loved me unconditionally. Nobody up to then, other than my children, had loved me so much. Why did God love me like this? I was a nobody, an ordinary person. Who was this God?

I heard about a man who did what they called 'deliverance courses' for people. I have no idea why I joined his class on a Wednesday night in early 2003, but I did. I did not believe I had anything that needed cleaning out of me. The man's name was Robert Lindsay, and I went faithfully to every one of his classes. All I remember learning was that no matter what you had done or what you had been through, Jesus had the power to take away any problem or addiction you had. Let me tell you that I had no intention of stopping smoking. This was my enjoyment in life and that was that. Case closed. Anyway, we had to pray and write whatever was revealed to us by the

Holy Spirit in a journal. I did this faithfully – and never read it back.

After the course was over, we had to have a one-on-one with Rob and his wife and some other church member. In early March 2003 it was my turn for the one-on-one session and I puffed cigarettes all the way to his house.

I have to say that what happened that day changed my life forever. I found the father I had never had. I found the father I had spent my entire life seeking. He was right there all the time but I was too stupid to see him. My father, my *abba*, my daddy. I never had a flesh father, but I found God the Father, and that was unbelievable.

We went through all I had written down then prayed about it, and I had to breathe these curses and addictions out of me. I cried like I had never cried in my life. I had spent most of my life crying, but not like this, this was strangely different. Robert Lindsay told me I had been cured from the addiction of nicotine and I told him I didn't think so. I said the first thing I would do when I climbed in my car was light a cigarette, and he said of course I would, because I had not yet realized what God had done for me.

I went home mentally exhausted and lay on my bed for three days crying and fighting God. On the thirteenth day of March, 2003, Rob phoned me and asked how I was doing, and I told him I was doing very badly, and these were his words to me: 'God never started you smoking, you started you smoking. God has done 99 per cent of the work for you. Are you telling me that you can't honour him with 1 per cent effort? All you have to do is break the habit of holding a

cigarette in your hand. That's all God has left for you to do.'
I have never, thanks to God, ever touched a cigarette again.
That is how God's power works.

That was my first lesson in learning that when we get
serious with God, God gets very serious about us. I can never
try to take any of this glory for myself. I had stopped smoking
and God had to be glorified for it.

10

The Kidz Club

I kept asking God why. Why did I have to give up smoking? I had enjoyed it, and I felt I hurt no one by doing it. Slowly God started to reveal His plan to me.

At Cambridge Baptist we are blessed with many opportunities to learn about God. On a Friday afternoon, various age groups met to have fun and learn about Jesus at the same time. A beautiful young lady, Lennae Clur, was running Kidz Club for three- to eight-year-olds from 3 p.m. to 4 p.m. She approached me and asked if I would consider coming to help her on a Friday. I immediately said no, as I didn't think this was for me.

Well, God had other plans. Lennae approached me once more, and I felt so bad about saying no again I said OK, I would come on the following Friday and see what it was all about.

Well, what an experience. I walked in and instantly fell in love with all these little faces. I was hooked. I started going every Friday and began to feel a deep love for these children.

After some months, Lennae fell very sick and never came back to Kidz Club. I had to now take over the club! 'No way, Lord, can I do this,' I said. 'What if I teach these children wrong things about You? Who is going to teach me? No, Lord, I am really very sorry, but I can't do this. No way is this even a possibility for me. No, Lord, *no*.'

God kept saying to me that He would help me. He would equip me. He kept saying He had chosen me and I just had to be faithful to Him. I kept saying, 'I'm a dirty sinner and I cannot be given this huge responsibility of teaching these children!' At that stage there were about twenty to thirty children attending this class.

Eventually I said to myself, 'OK, you can do this, Pauline. One Friday at a time.'

I could not pray in front of people, but here I could learn how to pray, as these little children never ever judged me. I started to grow as a Christian, as I could make mistakes with the children and they just loved me more. It wasn't only me that was growing; the children started to grow in numbers. We were sometimes more than 100. I had been blessed with helpers. This was a special time for me as most of these children just wanted a hug or a kiss, or to just tell you their problems or joys from the day. We had fun. We were all learning about Jesus from a child's level. I never believed I was good enough to teach children about Jesus because I was such a sinner, and yet Jesus believed in me.

God also knew I needed to be jumping and singing and playing with the children and couldn't be concentrating on smoking or be coughing every time we ran around. God can see the big picture. We cannot.

A girl called Candy started coming to Kidz Club with me and began to learn about Jesus, enjoying it more and more. I was asked to give a talk at the older group and Candice Grotjohn came along to listen. She gave her life to the Lord that night. I spoke on the death of my brother, and Pastor John Koning commented that that group of children usually behaved as if they were on drugs and yet everyone sat quietly and listened to my talk. It felt good. I enjoyed 'working for Jesus'. Candy was an only child. It can be hard for children with no brothers and sisters to learn to share with others, but Candy's mother, Leeanne, told me that she was so grateful that her daughter came into my family as she really learnt to share and to give. She gave her clothes to the needy, sent monetary donations to the soup kitchen as she was not able to assist in person, prayed for people needing prayer and was involved over Christmas-time with the buying and making up of hundreds of parcels for the children in East London who did not get a present for Christmas.

I finished taking the club in the February of 2011, just before I left South Africa for the UK. I told the children I would be back with them by August, as I believed this to be true. I didn't know God had other plans for me.

But I know it is right here for me to tell you more about Lennae. So here, in a chapter of her own, is her story.

11

Lennae's Story

Written by her mother, Cherry Clur

Lennae, our third daughter, was born on 5 January 1985, a month earlier than expected, so she took us by surprise when we were on a camping holiday. Edmund, her dad, had to be called away from his fishing to welcome her into the world. Her two big sisters, Michelle (five) and Carolyn (three) were very happy to have a live little doll to play with!

At school she managed to do quite well, although she seemed to put very little effort into learning – she said she listened well in class so she did not have to study so hard at home. She was relaxed and easy-going by nature. Apart from having allergies, she was a well and healthy child, and she enjoyed life. At high school she took Art as a subject, and she loved her pottery classes. All over our home we still have pottery objects that she made, each one different, unique and special – just like our three girls.

At the age of thirteen she was baptized to show everyone that she was a Christian and had accepted Jesus as her Saviour. This does not mean that she was perfect. As a teenager, she tested my patience many times by being very untidy. Often her bedroom looked as if a bomb had hit it, and she was quite happy for it to stay that way. She has a poster on her door which read: 'It's my mess and I like it'.

Lennae always loved children, and naturally wanted to teach them. She started with teaching pre-schoolers in Sunday school when she was fifteen years old. At the age of sixteen she took over the running of Whirlybirds at the church on Friday afternoons. This was a Bible club for children aged three to eight, and she changed the name to Kidz Club. She loved God and wanted to share His love with all those children. She especially had a soft spot for children who came from troubled homes. From a young age she used to tell me that she would probably run a children's home one day, or adopt a large number of children – when she married a rich farmer!

Lennae was very involved in the youth work at Cambridge Baptist Church. She helped to make the coffee bar become a place where the young people could meet, and she got her dad to build the veranda roof for it. As a surprise for her, he had someone put the words 'Coffee Bar' in lights on the outside wall. Unfortunately she did not get to see the surprise because she went to heaven a few days before it was put up.

Lennae's school friends remember her as the one they could confide in and turn to when they had problems. She was always caring and understanding. I remember hearing her give 'motherly' advice on the phone to some of them, and it surprised me that she had the wisdom to say the right thing at the right time. She was not a leader, but was always in the background, supporting those who were in the limelight.

After finishing matric, Lennae studied for a Diploma in Educare. She needed a certain number of hours of practical experience, so she listed all the Sunday school teaching, Kidz Club work, holiday clubs and short-term missions trips she had taken part in. She also worked at Little Oaks Educare as a teacher.

On Saturday afternoons we went with a group of volunteers to an orphanage called House on the Rock, where we told Bible stories to about sixty children and played with them. In December 2008, Lennae wanted to give each child a Christmas gift – a cushion – that was their own, because all the children there shared clothes and toys. She organized donations and got many church people involved in making the cushions. Just before Christmas, each child received a unique cushion to decorate their bed or cot. It had their name and an appropriate picture on it. She told them that it was to remind them that they were 'special individuals and God loved them'.

On 30 July 2004 Lennae collapsed while she was teaching at Little Oaks. She was nineteen years old. We rushed her to hospital and were told she had suffered a brain haemorrhage (a stroke) and she was 'lucky to be alive'. We asked the church to pray for her, and although her right side had been paralyzed, she got up and walked a short distance after five days. The weeks after that were very difficult for all of us, because she could not stand loud noises or bright lights. We all stayed in a dark, quiet house while she slowly recovered. She could not read or write at that stage, so her studies were just put aside. We called her our 'survivor'. Later, she called this 'miracle number one'. We were so grateful that the Lord had answered our prayers for her.

One month later when she was still very weak and partially lame on her right side, Lennae got a terrible pain in her chest. I took her to the doctor, and while she was having X-rays taken, her lung collapsed on her left side – she was suffocating – and we almost lost her again. She had emergency surgery, but after that her lung could not inflate because it was leaking air into her chest cavity. After two weeks, the specialist decided to operate on her lung. This was a major operation – they cut her chest open from front to back. I spent every day with her at the hospital for almost a month, because she could not use either of her arms. She suffered with terrible pain after the operation and not even morphine helped for long. The staples around half her body made it very difficult for her to move or do anything for herself.

I became a full-time nurse once she came home. It was terrible to see her suffering so much. All of us did whatever we could to make her more comfortable. Slowly she started to recover, and after a few months she learnt to write and move around on her own again. A specialist told us that she had Marfan syndrome, but it did not mean much to us then. We were so grateful that she was alive.

In December that year, Lennae underwent brain surgery to correct the malformation of blood vessels that had caused her stroke. This was a very stressful time for all of us because there were no guarantees that she would be totally 'normal' afterwards. Hundreds of people were praying, and God answered our prayers for her again. It was another miracle that she came through that operation with very few after-effects. In July of 2005 she wrote about her memories of that time, called *Within a Year*, where she gave thanks to God for the three miracles He had worked in her life. She ended by writing: 'I know that I am His child and He knows what is best for me and will do it in His timing.'

At that time I thought that I had just experienced the worst year of my life. It was terrible to watch my daughter suffer so much, and I could not stop any of it from happening. Many times I wished that I could take the pain for her. My prayer life became more intense as all I could do was trust God to give me the strength to help her. The previous year our Bible study group had done the course called: 'The testing of your faith'. We learnt that God allows bad circumstances and trials in our lives to test what we really believe about Him and to help us mature as Christians. This was a series of huge tests for me and my family.

I am so thankful that God carried us through that year. It was because so many people were praying for Lennae and for all of us. It is only in times of crisis that you fully appreciate how blessed you are to be part of a huge family who love and support you. We also have the added blessing of being part of an enormous Christian family. We are forever grateful to them all.

In between Lennae's two operations that year, she wrote a few more exams and received her Diploma in Educare. She had missed a semester of lectures, and she could not read much after the stroke, so Michelle and I read her notes to her and taught her enough to pass. God answered prayer.

She then decided to study through UNISA (University of South Africa) to become a qualified teacher! I knew that she might only live a short life, but I kept that information, given to me from the specialist, to myself, and we did not talk about Marfan syndrome – we did not really believe that she had it because she was a 'survivor'. The doctor told her she could do anything except kick-start a Boeing! I could not stop her from doing what she had set her heart on. I could only support her and pray that the Lord would keep her well and strong.

To earn money, she looked after a little boy called Kyle, from when he was four months old until he turned two. She was delighted to be his 'day mummy', and she loved him as if he was her own child. When he was sick she would phone me to ask what to do for him, and then she would relay that information to his mother. I knew that she would probably not be able to have her own children, so I was so glad that she could have that experience.

During those years of studying, Lennae had to do a lot of practical assignments. She had to make gym equipment, educational toys and many pictures and charts. Michelle, Carolyn and I often got involved in helping her to make, sew, paint or colour these teaching aids. Sometimes Edmund also helped, making things for her in the garage. She had to send photos of these items to UNISA and get a teacher to look at them and verify that they were home-made and 'real'.

In her third year of studying, Lennae practised teaching at a number of schools. After working for three weeks at the Abbotsford Christian School, they asked her to teach a class there even though she did not have her degree yet. She declined the offer because she wanted to put all her effort into her studies.

She also had practical experience in teaching at Hudson Park Primary School, and they asked her to become a teacher aid in a pre-school class. She took that job and loved it. When that teacher was very sick, Lennae taught her class for seven weeks. I could see how extremely exhausted she was when she came home in the afternoons, and she collapsed on her bed for two hours of sleep. I used to wonder if she would have enough strength to be a full-time teacher...

On 22 April 2009, Lennae travelled to Johannesburg with three guys from the church, to attend a Baptist youth conference for youth leaders. I was very uneasy about her going so far away from home, knowing that she was not really well – I prayed all weekend that she would stay well and safe. She thoroughly enjoyed the conference and the whole trip, and I was very thankful when she arrived home safely on the Tuesday.

A few weeks before that she had given her testimony at a Friday night youth meeting. We were told that she had spoken about her problems and had thanked God for saving her physically and spiritually. She made it clear that Jesus had saved her from the consequences of her sin, and she knew she would go to heaven when she died.

Michelle and Carolyn remember spending a lovely evening with Lennae and a group of girls from the church on Thursday, 30 April 2009. They played games and laughed for hours – their last happy memories with her.

The next day, Friday, was Lennae's last day with us. It was the 1 May – a public holiday – and the church youth had planned to do outreach activities with the children at a place called Garcia Flats. Lennae was one of the leaders, so she went there early that morning to play games and do 'fun things' with them. I received an SMS from her at about lunchtime to say that she was having lunch with the other leaders and friends.

She rushed home to change, and then went to Cabin Club at the church (for nine- to twelve-year-olds) because some of the children had begged her to come. While she was playing duster hockey with the kids, she suddenly got a bad pain in her back and she started battling to breathe. A friend brought her home and I dosed her up and told her to rest. The pain got worse and I decided to take her to the emergency room at St Dominic's Hospital. After X-rays were taken, the doctors said she had a 'potentially fatal' condition, but they did not know exactly what the problem was. They decided to operate on her and sent her by ambulance to the East London Private Hospital for more tests and X-rays.

My mother, Michelle and Carolyn were there and we saw Lennae briefly in the Intensive Care Unit before they took her to theatre. We prayed with her and assured her that we loved her. I reminded her that she was our 'survivor' and my last words to her were: 'See you in the morning.' Some friends from church had arrived at the hospital too because a message had gone out asking people to pray for her. Her friends wrote notes to her, but she did not get a chance to read them.

Edmund was at Cebe for the weekend and we battled to get a message to him to come home because the cell phone reception there is not good. He left Cebe as soon as he got the message, but it takes three hours to drive home, so he did not get a chance to see our daughter before she went into theatre. After he arrived at the hospital, at about 11.30 p.m., a nurse told us to all go home because they were still preparing to operate and the operation could take up to five hours. She said that she would call us when there was any news. My mother and Michelle went home with us and we all went to bed, but not to sleep.

At about 2 a.m. the phone rang. The nurse said we needed to come to the hospital. We drove back there in silence, dreading what we might hear. A specialist explained to us that they had called other specialists in to assist – two had driven down from King William's Town so there were five altogether. They were prepared to do heart bypass surgery if necessary, but when they opened up Lennae's chest, they found that there was nothing that could be done to save her life. She had suffered a massive aneurysm and her blood vessels were too weak to operate on because of Marfan syndrome.

It is impossible to describe how you feel when you are told that your daughter, or sister, or granddaughter has just died. Disbelief, shock, questions, regrets, anger, hurt, sorrow and pain flash through your mind immediately and for many months or even years afterwards.

Again our family and church family carried us in prayer through the very dark days and weeks that followed. From all over East London, South Africa and other countries, messages of sympathy and love poured in. We also received so much practical help during that time. Hudson Park Primary School teachers brought us meals for two weeks. Many of them did not even know us. We received hundreds of cards and letters – the support was overwhelming.

About 400 people attended the memorial service – the church was overflowing. Our pastor preached about eternity and the fact that we all need to prepare for life after death by getting right with God before it is too late. We found out afterwards that many people had been challenged by the message that day.

We thank and praise the Lord that Lennae's life had made an impact on so many people – young and old – during her lifetime and in her death.

People donated money in lieu of flowers to the church youth ministry, and we were able to buy two large table and bench sets to go outside the youth coffee bar, in memory of Lennae. A Hudson Park mother also donated an outside bench to the school in memory of her. We are so grateful for these things.

I believe that at the age of twenty-four, Lennae had completed the work God wanted her to do on earth. I came to accept her death quite early on, and God gave me a sense of peace through those early weeks because I knew that she was in heaven with Him. I was grateful that she was not suffering physically anymore. I knew that her biggest fear was having another big operation and feeling the pain of having staples all over her body again. She just went to sleep in theatre. Her last day could have been far more traumatic for her and all of us around her, but God spared us from that.

She was not more special to us than our other two daughters, but she left a big gap in our family. We all went through times of deep depression and we still feel the loss today. The hurt of bereavement stays with you, but as time goes on, you learn to handle it better. We eventually learnt to laugh again, and our great comfort is that we will see Lennae in heaven one day. I can picture her there – playing happily, with a huge crowd of children around her. Thank You, heavenly Father!

Lennae

Pastor George Dennison was asked to write a tribute to Lennae in the Church Newsletter. The following words are extracts of what he wrote:

2 Timothy 4:7 says: 'I have fought the good fight, I have finished the race, I have kept the faith.' We usually apply the words of this text to elderly people who have made significant contributions to various fields of Christian ministry. I believe they apply to Lennae too …

We remember her enthusiasm in all she did for the Lord, and for others. Who will forget the compassion she showed, her infectious smile, her bright and happy disposition, and the friendliness to, and concern for, everyone, irrespective of their age. The impact of all she did increases as we remember that she had not enjoyed the best of health over the past five years ...

The impact of her love for her Lord, for her family and for all of us, has left indelible impressions on our lives, and we are grateful for every memory ...

'Precious in the sight of the LORD is the death of his saints' (Psalm 116:15 KJV), and we believe the Lord said, 'Welcome home, Lennae, you were a good and faithful servant.'

12

Losing My Mother

One Sunday Rob Lindsay invited me to attend one of his services. As I went in, the strangest thing happened to me. I saw myself walking in carrying loads of baggage all strapped to my shoulders. My shoulders where stooped forward from the weight of what I dragged around with me. Mountains of baggage went into that service with me.

Then God clearly showed me how He was taking all that baggage away from me. He cut the straps holding the weight and allowed me to walk out of that church, free! I kept hearing the words 'And the truth will set you free'. I had no idea what this meant and eventually came across it in my Bible in John 8:32: 'Then you will know the truth, and the truth will set you free.' His Word is the Bible, and it will set me free. Jesus is the Word; He called Himself the truth. Therefore Jesus sets us free.

One thing He has taught me is not to put limits on Him. Our God is big, way bigger than us or our problems. This is how gracious our God is. I am still not where I would like to be, but He is not finished with me yet. He is still teaching me and showing me how to learn and how to grow in Him. I am still trying daily to just do His will.

I have been a Christian since 2000 now and feel as though I am still on baby formula when it comes to God! I really want to move on to soft foods with Him. But God's timing is different to ours. He knows the plans He has for us, as Jeremiah 29:11 tells us. No matter who we are or what we have done or what we have been through, God loves us. Yes, we are sinners, yet He loves us so much that He is willing to spend time on us, changing us, moulding us.

Something hit me the other day. It was that God uses a particular mother to be with a particular father to be able to make a certain child. He plans our DNA, characters and personalities. This was weird for me to imagine. Then I thought back to my life of hell with ASJ. God needed ASJ to make my four perfect, beautiful children. Not long after the twins came home from the hospital, I was taken away from that life. Seems surreal I know, but when you look at the bigger picture you start to see a pattern of how our God works. Start putting your own life into a picture form and look for God in everything and you will see He is there. I am slowly starting to see that we are on earth to glorify God and not glorify ourselves! I am beginning to realize it is in fact not about us and all about God; yet He loves us so much He wants us to be healthy, happy, prosperous, peaceful, joyful, and to love and try to help whoever we can.

So, I was changing. Very slowly, but it was there. I didn't enjoy partying anymore, and drinking had lost its fun. I could even walk into places on my own now. The Holy Spirit was making me confident. I need to stress the fact that I'm not perfect. I still think evil things and do ugly things. I still have a cruel tongue, though not as bad as it used to be. But I am a daughter of the King, a child of His grace – His free favour – and, as they say, a work in progress.

But 2003 was also a very sad year for me. My mother was diagnosed with cervical cancer. I have never been able to understand why my mother did not use the medical aid that she paid so much money monthly towards. She never said a word about the bad infection she had. I used to visit her two to three times a week and maybe she felt I was too busy for her. My visits where not long ones. My life was always hectic, rushing all the time.

My mother and I had a secret war going on our entire lives. I hated the fact that she drank and battled to come to terms with it. My sisters always told me I was too hard on her, that I must remember the difficult life she had had. I could never accept this excuse.

Just after I stopped smoking, one Saturday morning I took a walk to my mother's house and found her in a semi-coma. I phoned for an ambulance to take her to St Dominic's Hospital and then rang Leslie in King William's Town. I went home, got my car and raced to the hospital. After my mother had been examined by a specialist, Leslie and I were called in to see him. He told us that in his opinion, my mother would not make it through the night. I sobbed and begged God to give me a chance to make my wrongs into rights with my mother. How could God take my mother before I had asked for her forgiveness? I spent that night on the floor and was never so cold in all my life. Leslie slept in the chair. At around four in the morning I heard my mother call me. She asked me where she was and what was going on.

God gave me three more months with my mother. Three months to nurse her, to love her unconditionally, three months for forgiveness, three months of what it felt like to have a sober mother. What a three months. How can I ever thank God for this time? Precious time in which I could make all my wrongs into rights. My family didn't see much of me and John said a lot of ugly things to me but I didn't care about anything except my mother. I lost so much weight that I looked like a bag of bones. There was no time to eat. Only time to be with my mother. We forgave each other, and we spoke a lot about God and Brendon and Colleen.

The hospice were called in and they started administering morphine to her. That seemed to be the end when the morphine started. She kept asking me to please not let her go to heaven on her own. Please would I be there to hold her hand. That was my mother's final request to me and one I never managed to keep. She was eventually moved into the hospice, as the end was near. I would sit with her from about six in the morning to around eight, then I would rush to work for two to three hours, then race back to sit with my mother until twelve, one o'clock in the morning, then go home and shower and sleep for a few hours, then get up again at five and start the same daily routine. She seemed to be in a permanent coma now, when she suddenly opened her eyes and called me. She said she wanted to thank me so much for loving her and looking after her. I answered that it had been the greatest honour of my life and I would not leave her. This happened on the Thursday, and just before I arrived to be with her on the Friday morning, she left to be with Jesus. That was 11 July 2003. I was fifteen minutes too late to keep my word to her.

But although I had lost my mother, I still had my children, and my church. I cannot thank God enough for leading me to Cambridge Baptist Church because it feels as though God handpicked these people for my life. They showed so much love, so much compassion, I actually can't find the words to describe them, except to say that they have been part of God's plans for my life.

In my experience, having invited people to attend church, the excuses are always the same: 'The people don't make me feel welcome.' Well, I also used those excuses. How else do you get out of going to church? But I want to know my Father more. I want to know what His plans for my life are. How can I glorify my Father? I won't know if I don't spend time with Him. The saddest part for me, going to church, was that my children stopped going.

Kerri was a border swimmer from Grade One. She could swim unbelievably well. I was always so proud to sit and watch her swim using the butterfly stroke, as no one could keep up with her. Kerri thought she was one of the boys, but I think she just woke one morning and realized that she was a girl! She was always very shy and, like me, battled to go places on her own. After I started to deal with my fears, I started to try to help her with hers.

As the oldest, I would expect more from her than I would the boys. I would always shout at her and boss her around. It was only when I started to surrender to Jesus, and He began to control my life that I realized how hard on her I was. How do you make wrongs into rights with children? She knows how much I love her. She knows how much I sacrificed for her. She knows how hard I worked for her. Yet in human terms I still failed her. I asked God to forgive me, and to help me, and this was what God did.

He brought a wonderful man into Kerri's life, who has been helping her where I failed. God is, at the time of writing, pouring blessings into Kerri's life. She has a beautiful home, she has a nice car, she stays at home and takes care of my grandchildren. She is brilliant with baking and decorating cakes. I watch her create these tiny, perfect cake decorations, and have no idea how she does it.

My three sons... right from when they were small, they received all the attention, as they looked like triplets. Same size, little blondies. Everywhere we went these boys would be stopped and spoken to. Shawn was always one grade ahead of his brothers. All Shawn ever wanted to do was play rugby and so the twins followed. Whatever Shawn said or did was what happened. They all played first team rugby from an early age in high school and were very popular both with teachers but also with the students. In 2007, Shawn became head boy for Cambridge High School and I nearly died with pride. That October at prize-giving, Shawn handed his head boy badge over to his brother Jason. Well, I cried like a baby. In one family there were two head boys, and my darling Justen was a prefect. So God has definitely given these three boys leadership qualities.

As you can hear, I am very proud of my four children, or should I say, the great loves of my life. Shawn has qualified as an electrician and now wants to study further. Jason and

Justen have qualified as plumbers and are trying to save so they can start their own business one day. I pray only great success into their lives.

Just to finish this chapter, I want to tell you about what I call the 'forgotten children', Colleen's daughter and son. Forgotten for so many years, left to try to fend for themselves, battling along in life and never complaining... I thank God for giving me the chance to make amends in these children's lives. I have asked them both to forgive me for all the years of silence and without hesitation they both said, 'We forgave you a long time ago.' Why can they forgive me so easily and yet I battle to forgive myself? God has given me the chance to start making all my wrongs into rights. I know I will never be able to fix all my wrongs in a night, but at least I am working on them now. I pray that God have mercy on the children and bless them both in a huge way. Nothing is impossible with God. I have to constantly remind myself that God's time is not like our time.

Colleen's daughter got married and has had a beautiful little boy. I have been given the great honour of being this little boy's grandmother in place of my sister. I just pray I get it right this time round. Second chances are not for messing up.

13

Suicide

John made it very clear after we got married that he was not responsible for my children. They were my responsibility. He earned a good salary but would only pay the bond on the house and the medical aid. He felt I was responsible for all other monthly expenses. I earned a small salary and had to make it stretch so far that most months I couldn't breathe for debts. My children alone needed more than I was earning, not to mention all the other expenses, including the electricity, food, plus all the other little hidden costs that sneak up on us that we never expected.

I never received any maintenance from ASJ, and life was nothing but a struggle. I used to watch John go out drinking and gambling almost daily and barely had enough food to feed my children. Where was the fairness in life? When the children were very young I had tried to take ASJ to court for maintenance that he owed me, and to get monthly maintenance from him. I arrived at the East London court convinced I would be getting money and left in shock and tears. ASJ was such a fantastic liar that he even had the judge believing his lies. The judge threw the case out, as ASJ had lied so convincingly that he was unemployed that the judge took his word over that of my children's needs. I rushed home, got the proof I needed, and rushed back to the court. I showed them the evidence but was told that I should open a case of perjury against him. I drove home sobbing. My little children and I had nobody to turn to.

The electricity bills had become too much for me, and the children and I started sharing one bath every second day. We all hated this, but nobody said anything and we just got on quietly with life. It was when the boys were in grade seven I had had enough. I went to a lady lawyer, and after some months she managed to help me and my children and had a garnishee order attached to ASJ's salary, forcing him to pay me R500 for each child every month. I felt rich. My children slowly started getting things. We started having baths every day. The struggle was so much less.

Then one afternoon there was a knock at the front door. When I opened it there stood a tall lady. She looked me up and down, and asked me why I stayed with John when I could get a good man. I had no idea what she was talking about. She told me how John was at her hotel every single day, and he and one of the bar ladies were very familiar with each other. He was taking her out for driving lessons, and when her children walked into the bar he bought them cold drinks, chocolates, chips and biltong (a dried, cured meat). We at home barely had any food! I was so angry and hurt.

He hurt me again and again, but I just closed my eyes. I started getting very bitchy towards him; he could say some very cruel things. The week before my mother died, he looked at me and said, 'When is your effing mother going to die, or is she going to spoil another weekend for me?' Cruel. Yip. People that knew him very well, if they are truly honest with themselves, will agree to what I am saying and no, I am not trying to bad-mouth him. It is past. I'm trying to show you what I kept putting up with.

When we were doing the alterations to the house I had wanted a door moved. I got my boys to help me to unscrew the screws that were very tight. My garden helper came to try to assist us. He took a huge screwdriver and started pushing to try to loosen the screws, and Justen bent over in front of him, watching to see if the screws would move. The screwdriver slipped and went into my boy's eye. I was ill with fright and rushed him straight to hospital. They performed an emergency operation to try to save the eye but the vision had been badly damaged. John screamed at me for being so negligent, and said I would have to live with the knowledge that I had blinded my son for life. I live with this guilt but I know that one day I will forgive myself for what I allowed to happen. Even though it was an accident, I should have seen the danger. I am slowly dealing with my guilt issues.

John became retrenched and spent months at home barely leaving the house. He would ask me to go to the library to get books for him and would mark them with a tiny J so I knew if he had read them or not. I never gave this much thought as was so overwhelmed with not losing my home. One day my boss' son told me he knew something about my husband that I did not know. When I questioned him, one thing led to another and I discovered that John had been having an affair. He told me to go and see the man John worked with. I went straight down to the company and asked the man why John had been retrenched. He told me that they had CCTV footage of John in the toilet every day with one of the cleaning ladies. Apparently John would whistle and this was the signal for her to go to the toilet with the pretence of cleaning it. I was devastated. Everybody knew except me. I stopped sleeping with him at this stage.

He had two children, and his son he clearly adored, but he never had much to say about his daughter. I think she knew how he felt about her as I read an email the ex-wife sent him after the daughter had had a baby. In the email she said that they wanted nothing more to do with him and for years he never really cared. They did eventually make friends again.

Colleen's little boy used to come to the house every day after school and I only found out last year why he suddenly stopped coming. His mother had just died, and he was always at our house with his cousins when apparently John called him and told him to 'eff off' to his gran and stop eating our food. I never even bothered to go to the little boy and find out why he wasn't coming to us anymore. I just thought he wanted to go to his little school friend more. How could I have not seen?

I can go on and on and on telling you stories, but this is enough for you to get the picture of how my life was.

About a year after my mother died, I wanted a divorce. John made all sorts of promises to me; he even started going to church. He gave his life to the Lord and was baptized. He really did change. He stopped drinking and gambling and just became a really nice person. I fell in love with him all over again. Life was so good for about four years, but on the evening of Kerri's twenty-first birthday party, he started drinking again. Things quickly went downhill from there. We took a huge bond out on the house; the excitement of my home improvements kept my mind occupied.

In 2010 the company I was working for closed down. So I had no job and no money. John started drinking and gambling very heavily and we got deeper and deeper into debt. It was around this time that God kept waking me up to write this book. It was also at this time that I discovered I was entitled to a British passport, as my father was British. We decided between the two of us that this was the best thing I could do to make money to help us. I explained to John that I would be sending the money I earned to my son's account so as to help him with the temptation of gambling. He agreed with me.

God opened this door for me to go to the UK. I cried every day to go back home. I kept getting phone calls from my children to say the bond on the house had not been paid, and the money I had saved to buy a ticket home had to be sent to them. Shawn had been taking videos of John eating from the floor as he was too drunk to sit at the table and eat. I was shattered. I was crying rivers every day, pleading with God to let me just go home. But I had no money for a ticket. In March 2011, just before I left South Africa, I felt as though God had given me the verse from Jeremiah 29:11:

For I know the plans I have for you,' declares the LORD, 'plans to prosper you and not to harm you, plans to give you hope and a future.

I clung to this promise day and night, crying, begging, pleading, but it seemed to fall on deaf ears. In June, Kerri phoned me to tell me she was pregnant, and what should have been a joyful time was only sad for me. 'Why, Lord, why?' No answers came. There was terrible fighting over money in the September, with John phoning me, drunk. I told him when he had sobered up about a week later that I was done with him. I flew home in the beginning of December, having no idea of what hell was awaiting me.

As it was almost Christmas, I couldn't get an appointment with a lawyer as most of them were closed until the middle of January. My appointment was made for Thursday, 19 January 2012. Christmas was fairly pleasant without John around. No shouting or drunkenness, just wonderful peace.

He returned on the afternoon of 31 December. He had been phoning Jason every day, saying he wished he was home with us. I was angry when he walked in, as I had planned a nice quiet evening at home alone. I attacked him, asking him why he was back, and then he walked out to go drinking.

John had caused so much trauma and devastation, that all I had was anger and hate towards him and could not talk nicely. I just shouted every time he tried to speak to me. I admit, I was horrible to him. I wanted him out of my life.

On Sunday, 15 January 2012, John woke me early to say he was going to Dimbaza, where he worked; he wanted to take some things there. I shouted at him for waking me up and I shouted at him to stop calling me his 'lovey'. Later that morning I made a big Sunday roast and he ate a lot, even asked for seconds, but as Justen said to me later, he was like a ghost walking around very quietly this day. After lunch he went and had a lie-down and got up again around 6 p.m. He made some tea and asked Justen to go to the shop for him. He then went to the bedroom and closed the door. When Justen got back from the shop, he took him what he had gone to buy for him, and John was lying in bed, reading. That night, my last thought before going to sleep was, 'Please, Lord, make this ugliness stop.' I was not sleeping properly and woke a couple of times every night, but not this night. I slept deeply and peacefully.

On the Monday morning, 16 January 2012, I said goodbye to the boys as they left, and went for a run. I think I was gone for about an hour and a half. On my return, I had a shower, and as I started down the passageway to get dressed, I suddenly felt cold. It dawned on me that John's pick-up truck was on the driveway, so where was he? I thought maybe he had had a flat tyre and a work colleague who lived locally had given him a lift, but as I made my way into the bedroom and glanced over at the dressing table I saw his wedding ring and papers. I knew in an instant what he had done.

I started screaming and my domestic worker, Lillian, and I started running. I knew where I would find him and was screaming as I ran. There he was, lying in the carport behind the car. I tried to run to him but somehow I couldn't get there.

Lillian went to him and said, 'He has a pillow on his face.' He had shot himself.

I clearly remember not being able to breathe. I tried and tried but could not get air into my lungs. I think I was screaming for my friend Barbara who lived across the road, but I'm not really sure what I was doing. My children all got a text message from me which made no sense.

I don't recall much after this. I have been told a lot by my family and I am slowly starting to regain my memory. I stopped remembering people's names for about two years. I do recall lying on the couch in the lounge and hearing one of my sons sobbing brokenly outside.

John's daughter from his first marriage phoned and told me children if I turned up at his funeral, they would have me arrested. There was such bad feeling. On Friday, 20 January 2012, my wonderful pastor at the time, John Koning, gave us a memorial service so that we could have a form of closure. John Koning gave me so much support after John died. He will always hold a very special place in my heart as a man who truly does what the Bible says – 'look after orphans and widows in their distress' James 1:27. And this he did for many months following all the ensuing ugliness.

That very afternoon John's brother arrived with a long list of all the things they wanted. They didn't even wait to cremate the man. John had always told us this would happen when he died. All I kept praying was, 'Please Lord, get these people out my life. Please make all the ugliness go away.'

John had planned every detail of his suicide. He was a brilliant man who had a treasure of knowledge in his head. But I do believe he was also a very, very damaged man, and that the alcohol had severely impaired his thinking. He left me his wedding ring, together with a very unpleasant letter, praying that I would suffer for the rest of my life. He had always told me that if I ever tried to leave him he would shoot himself. He blamed my beautiful friend, Wendy Meier, for breaking up his marriage as she had been trying to help me find a house. You can see by this behaviour that there seemed to be a serious problem with his mind.

It was a nightmare. I would not wish this on another human soul. Phone calls. Shouting. Swearing. His daughter demanded all John's personal effects. I packed everything up in boxes for her. I found all his condoms and sex toys and pornographic movies and packed *everything* for them. Later that day I had his ex-wife screaming through the door, asking how could I send those things? But that was part of his personal effects. That was part of who he was. They never said to me, 'We only want his clean effects and you can have the dirty effects.' They had said they wanted everything, so I sent everything. To be honest, I probably wouldn't have done that today.

I was seeing a psychologist that my two pastors, John Koning and George Dennison, had referred me to. He said that I had been mentally abused for twenty years and the more I thought about it, the more I could see this. I had to get antidepressants from my doctor as I was having such severe panic attacks I couldn't leave the house. I seemed to be in a confused state of mind; I battled to focus and to understand the simplest thing. I couldn't eat or sleep; I just walked around the dark house all night. Sometimes I would sit in bed and look around me. It felt as though he was there watching me, waiting for me to sleep so he could strangle me. I was a complete mess.

My daughter came to me and said she was having terrible nightmares about John and felt threatened by him. One of my sons, who was usually fearless – he scared me because he was so fearless – said that every time he went to put the car away he felt fear in the front garden. And then another of my sons came to me and said he was scared. Something was going on in the house. One of my boys' gums had started bleeding. He would wake up with a mouth full of blood and his pillows were covered in blood. Lillian said she could not stay in the house alone anymore, John's presence seemed to be there, as if trying to kill hers. My dogs kept walking around and staring at places where he used to sit, and they would growl. It was scary. My parrot kept calling 'John' and talking to him. I was totally freaked out.

I sat on the bed in February 2012 and looked up and said, 'Lord, if You don't save me now, I'm going to die.' I could not stop crying, and the only time I slept was when I went to Kerri and her husband's house. I would just fall asleep on their couch.

This particular morning I went to the local shop out of desperation, as I had nothing left to eat in the house. As I went around a corner, I walked straight into my special friend, Tracey Bridger. I was babbling to her about what was going on in the house, and she said I was to leave it to her.

The following afternoon, two ladies and a man arrived at the house. They said they had come to help us. This was 29 February 2012, leap year. They started in my room and took me into my dressing room, which I had been terrified to go in to. One of the ladies looked at me and said I was to close my eyes. She asked me what I saw, and the weird part was, I was in the middle of the ocean and I was drowning.

She said, 'Look up and tell me what you see.'

I said, 'A helicopter and a rope.'

'That is Jesus. He is here to save you,' she said.

She had *no* idea that the morning before I had told Jesus that if He didn't save me, I would die. They all said there was a strong presence of 'something' in the room. They prayed and prayed, and made cross signs all over with oil. When they stepped into my son's room – the one who had the bleeding gums – the lady who had spoken to me held her arms up over her chest in a cross fashion and said, 'I'm battling to breathe in here.' They did not know that my son had had bleeding gums.

They prayed and went through the same rituals in every room in the entire house. They then prayed for us all. When they stepped out of the front door, the other lady, who hadn't said much at all, stopped and looked back and said she felt he had left the house on the morning of 16 January cursing me to hell.

They prayed and burnt his letter, and prayed over his ring. That night we all slept deeply. My son's gums never bled again. The dogs stopped growling. Lillian was happy to be alone at the house. If I had not witnessed this for myself, I would never have believed it. There was *something* in my home; a bad presence. While Christians do not believe that the spirits of dead people haunt the earth, they do believe in demonic forces, evil spirits, the enemy, that can possess and oppress. These spirits can even impersonate people so you think what you are dealing with is the 'ghost' of the dead person.

I felt the enemy had gone, but over Christmas 2014 we were all home and Kerri was awaked every night at 3 a.m. on the dot. My baby granddaughter would start screaming. It then came out that my son who slept in that room would also wake at 3 a.m. So I went and stood in the corner where they felt they could feel this 'presence' and said, 'My God is bigger than you will ever be. Put that in your pipe and smoke it.'

I did not ask God for any of John's pension, even though I was entitled to it. I only asked for my home. My lawyer at the time believed I deserved the pension, but I left it all in God's hands. I knew He would sort everything out for me. God gave me my house, completely bond-free! All I can say now is, 'Thank You, Jesus. I have freedom. I have peace.'

I have spent so much time trying to work out why God took me to the UK in the first place and I honestly believe that in 2011 it was to free me from John's hold over my life. The moment I had made up my mind with absolute certainty that I was divorcing him, the door opened for me to go home.

I want to explain to you what suicide did to us as a family. We all went through a time of disbelief, battling to come to terms with how a person could do this; the million questions one has and will never have answers to. All I kept asking was, 'Where is John now? What happened to him?' Every person I spoke to had a different version of what they believed.

I have always believed that if a person committed suicide then their soul would wander around for eternity never finding rest, but of course, that isn't a biblical view. This is what I read in the Bible – murder is a sin and suicide is the same as murder, as it is self-murder. God is very clear that He is the only one who can take a life. In Psalm 31:15 we read 'My times are in your hands', and in Job 1:21 we see Job declaring 'The LORD gave and the LORD has taken away' when he suffered great loss; truly, *the Lord* gives life and it is for *the Lord* to take it away. We cannot take God's authority upon ourselves and take our own lives. But God is a merciful God. I thought, 'What happened if John shouted out to Jesus just before he pulled the trigger to forgive him for his actions? What then?'

After his death, we as a family would all be googling 'suicide' day and night, reading all the different opinions on it. I think this only made us all the more confused. When I looked at the suicide statistics I was horrified at the totals.

Truthfully, I have had more than my fair share of times wishing I was dead. I have had the enemy, Satan, telling me on numerous occasions how bad I am and how I'm worthy of nothing pleasant, till all I can see is suicide as the answer. I know what hardship and pain is all about, but I was created for a reason and even though life is tough, I can't just quit. I know if I call on the name of Jesus He will save me. God will never lie to us or forsake us.

I still haven't made up my mind as to exactly where I think John is. But coming to terms with what he did is going to take me a lifetime to try to understand.

14

Working in Britain

Working in Britain has not been easy for me. Having to leave my family, friends, home, dogs, my church was a huge thing to do. When I first arrived in the UK I didn't know anybody except my friend Judy, and I didn't even know where she lived! I later realized that she was in Surrey, the same place my father had come from.

God had opened a door for me to come to Britain. I heard about an agency in Wales that trained live-in carers. I contacted them and flew over to Britain in the March of 2011. I went through the training with a group of other women who were also desperate to try to make a living, but one stood out in a big way – Busi. I felt so drawn to her. The agency I worked for owned a house just outside Abergavenny, and we all lived there whilst going through our training.

It was a terrible week for me as I was not only dealing with this huge change in my life, but the same day I arrived, Jason's girlfriend, Ashley's mother, Sandy, had a stroke. As she was so young I kept thinking she would probably take a few months to heal but would be just fine. But she died. All I wanted to do was to go home, but there was no money for a ticket back to South Africa. I felt so much pain and turmoil as I knew I was needed back home and had no way of getting there. I almost felt that God waited for me to leave as He knew I would never have got on that plane.

I had to try to focus on the training; it felt like my world was upside down, in a strange country with nobody. We finished our training on the Friday, and not all of us had work lined up. Before I even had time to worry about what was going to happen to me, Busi had loaded me up in her car and we travelled for hours up to her home in Blackburn. I cried most of the way. I remember her telling me that she had had no money and a cheque had arrived for her for £80, and that was when she knew that she had to take me home with her. God had given her money to take care of me until I started work.

Her husband and daughter just opened their house to me and told me to make myself at home. I do not believe I will ever receive such wonderful, humble hospitality again. These people had no idea who I was except I looked and acted like a crazy woman from South Africa and cried a lot! What a family.

I didn't know much about the agency I was with, and was really in need of work. On the Monday I received a phone call to say I was to start work on the Wednesday. The relief I experienced was unbelievable. Relief – and fear. I had no idea what to expect, working as a carer. That Wednesday morning in the pitch dark, Busi's husband took me to the station to start my journey to Bicester. It was with sadness that I left the home of Busi Grace Hlongwane, as I had felt so much love there. I remember sitting on the train wondering what on earth would happen to me now.

Working with people with Alzheimer's disease and other forms of dementia has been helping me to heal. It is a tough job, and one I still do at this present time, but I have found that God equips when He asks you to do things for Him. I have prayed daily for peace and patience and to just love these people who truly cannot help themselves. This is a terrible disease, and I have watched how the family members battle to accept what is happening to their loved ones. I have seen how a once very capable person slowly loses all ability to even do a simple task. I sometimes become overwhelmed with sadness and have often asked God not to allow this cruel disease to affect me.

Working with dementia patients, I have been threatened with a walking stick. I have been punched in the back, I have been locked in a kitchen, I have been accused of taking things. Most days consist of searching for some item or another. Things get hidden all the time and you waste a good part of the day searching. I used to get so frustrated as I couldn't understand the sense in wasting a good part of the day in searches, until I realized that I actually didn't have anything better to do! Every client is different. My main goal is kindness and love, lots of laughter and conversation, singing and dancing with some clients. I try to never argue or ask questions, and this is very, very difficult. As a carer, it is so important to make your client feel a sense of worth and to constantly keep their dignity. I often recite silently in my head, 'Do as though unto the Lord, Pauline.' I cope by telling myself that Jesus has brought me into this line of work for a reason and will take me out when He chooses. I could write a book on the experiences I have had as a carer alone! And I have made the most incredible friends in the UK.

If you look back over my life you will notice that Jesus has been there all along. When I believed I was alone, He was there, always waiting for me to call to Him. I remember one night at Bible study, our leader, Kobus Kotze, said, 'Yes, we all have big, powerful testimonies to say how Jesus came into our lives, but can you tell me what Jesus did for you today or even yesterday?' I have never forgotten these powerful words. Every day Jesus is with us, helping us.

I find life as a Christian very difficult, *but* far better than when I was not a Christian! I seem to have more 'enemy attacks' these days but I know I am not alone. I can hand my battles to Jesus. Every day I pray, read my Bible, and read my two devotional books. Every day I make time for Jesus because the moment I don't do this is when Satan attacks – when I am weak and not able to focus properly.

I arrived back in the UK early March 2015 and was very depressed to leave my daughter and grandchildren. I was angry that I had to come and work in Britain when I wanted to spend more time with them.

From the day I arrived, Satan started his attacks on me. The scary thing is, he knows what our weaknesses are and will use them to pull us down in life. Once we acknowledge what he is doing, we are able to fight back and hand everything over to Jesus. He catches me time and time again. I know his tricks so well, and yet they still trap me.

The worst attack I have ever experienced mentally is what I am about to tell you now. It took me seven weeks to wake up and realize what was going on. The moment I called out to Jesus to help me and save me I received a WhatsApp message from my friend, Ann. She had visions that Jesus had given her for me. I cried uncontrollably all that day. I was again saved by my God. He loves me absolutely and completely, never judging me but always forgiving my many sins. I do question why on earth He loves me so much – but I am His little girl. I am His child, and He loves me unconditionally. I tell myself I am not worthy of such great love. I do so many things that are wrong. But then I am reminded that this is exactly what the devil wants me to think. He wants me to fall. He wants me to stop praising Jesus. He wants me back so I cannot tell people how wonderful Jesus is. And I remind myself that Jesus loves us with our flaws and moods and ugliness and hurt and pain and confusion, and just keeps saying, 'Come to me … and I will give you rest' (Matthew 11:28).

The enemy does not want me to write this book and has tried many tactics to get me to stop, but I want to obey and glorify Jesus!

15

Attacks

For those of you who do not know what Tinder is, it's a dating site. My children decided it was time for their mother to start having a look at what was out there! At first I had absolutely no interest in finding a man but really enjoyed looking and reading all the various profiles.

As I told you, when I arrived back in the UK I was depressed as I wanted to be with my grandchildren and my daughter. Anyway, one afternoon I logged into Tinder and started going through faces. One face jumped out at me and I pushed the like/accept button and it immediately said I had a match. He had liked my picture earlier in the day.

Well, what can I say about Mr Tinder except that he hurt me very deeply? I tried to break contact with him three times and each time he convinced me that he was the real deal. Honest, loving, sincere, faithful, truthful – the entire wonderful package. I was besotted with this man. We messaged each other via WhatsApp for hours and hours and days and days. He kept saying he would drive to wherever I was, no problem, even just to see me for a few hours. He had me hook, line and sinker; he told me exactly what I wanted to hear, and I honestly believed that this was 'the one'.

The only thing that worried me – and I told him this – was that he wasn't a Christian, but I kept telling myself I could get him to learn to love Jesus. He said he would always support me in everything I did, but would not attend church with me. And I kept thinking, 'I can overcome this.'

I was hardly reading my Bible or messaging my children, as all I could think of was this man. I met him via Tinder on 7 March and it was all over on 7 April.

I hadn't heard from him in two days and found this very strange, as this man messaged me day and night, and now dead silence. Anyway, I convinced myself that he had been in a car accident and eventually phoned his mother out of desperation. She was very cold to me and said that he would contact me when he was ready. I asked her if she had heard from him, and she said no, she hadn't.

So I had to wonder how she knew he would 'contact me when he was ready' unless she had experienced other desperate phone calls.

A day later at 1 a.m. I got a message from him asking me how I had dared to contact his mother, and how it had taken him all night to calm her down. Anyway, I started to think that this was how he got his kicks out of life.

As women, I think we go on these dating sites in the hope of meeting a partner but we really must be very careful, because not everyone we meet will have good intentions. The Bible tells us we should guard our hearts (Proverbs 4:23). I met other men, and the last man I had anything to do with via messages was such a sweet man – or so it seemed. I had been so hurt by Tinder One that I wasn't sure I could do this again, and started begging God to remove him before I got hurt as I was really starting to like Tinder Two.

Three days later he cancelled a date. I was angry, then I was hurt, then I started telling myself, 'I'm worth nothing – I can't even find a date on a dating site!' But then I remembered that I had been asking God to not allow hurt into my life again.

It was then that I think I came back to my senses. I realized I wasn't reading my Bible or praying. All I was doing was begging God for mercy; begging and pleading with Him. Then, something strange happened. I went to the doctor for my antidepressant and my thyroid medication and the doctor said she wanted me to have a full blood count. I saw the nurse a week later and she took blood for a full blood count and suggested I was to have a smear to check that I was clear of any cancer.

A few days later, my client needed a strap for her glasses and the chemist didn't have any. The lady who served us suggested I go to the optician next door. We walked into the optician's and I ended up with an appointment for that afternoon to have my eyes checked. Back in the February in South Africa, my eye doctor had told me that he thought I may be developing glaucoma, and I had been a little tense about this. That afternoon I had my eyes examined and was told I had to go to the hospital for further tests. I really started panicking about not driving any longer, and prayed about this. I decided to not panic until I had been for the tests, and then to deal with the outcome. Sometimes this is easier said than done!

That very Friday saw me taken into the next big town by the groundsman to have all the necessary tests done. The outcome was that for now I was absolutely fine. A week later, a letter arrived in the mail to say I needed to have a bowel cancer test. Every test I had just undertaken came back all-clear. I had been given a clean bill of health, and now I started questioning, 'Why, Lord? What is it You are preparing me to do for You?'

I have learnt that nothing happens without a reason. I will understand all of this eventually. I do not believe in coincidences, I believe in Godincidences.

You may be asking why this Christian woman would join a non-Christian dating site, and I will be very honest with you. When my children added me on, I had absolutely no intention of ever really using it. It was merely a way to pass some time and to see what type of men were out there. It did not take me long to realize that if God wants a man in my life, then He will bring him and I do not have to go looking. I also want to say that I am human. I am made of flesh. I make daily mistakes and this is the reason I am so in need of God. I am fully aware I have been saved by grace and grace alone, which is unmerited favour. People seem to have this opinion that if you are a Christian then you don't do any things that are wrong, and this is so far from the truth. We are human but are striving to be like Jesus, which I'm sad to say not one of us will ever achieve until we get to heaven.

I then had this huge urge to start writing again. It had been five years and I hadn't touched this book, and now I was been told to start writing again. Once I knew that I was to begin writing again, the enemy attacks *really* started. I started getting messages from my family. Deep depression had set in for some of them. Kerri messaged me to say that 'John' was back and that she had had a vision. Kerri has from a very young age had dreams of certain things, and they always seemed to come true. When she dreamed, we as a family always got very nervous.

The message she sent me read: 'I was in the bathroom and looked up at the wall and suddenly got goose bumps all over my body. I saw Jesus' tomb and a man standing outside pointing at it and crying … I swear I looked [up] images and I found exactly what I had seen.' She had sent me the image. I had no idea what this meant, but my friend Tracey Bridger said she needed to pray and ask Jesus to reveal the meaning to her. This was when I knew we were in trouble, and needed more people praying for us. I find when I am weak and under attack I battle to pray and get strength. This is when I call on my prayer warriors to pray for me, and it doesn't take long and I'm up again and strong. I have learnt to confide in others and ask for help when I need it.

This particular day was a Saturday and I was sitting thinking about what I should do, feeling very down, when my phone beeped. It was a message from Ann, my missionary friend. This is what the message said: 'Pauline. You are being equipped for a walk that the Lord is going to ask you to take with Him. Be ready for a change.' With everything that was going on in my life, here was a clear message telling me to be ready. That entire afternoon Ann messaged me, encouraging me, praying over me, and all I did was cry. I cried and cried and cried and after more than two hours I felt completely drained, emotionally.

One thing that Ann had said was what I had been thinking of doing earlier, and that was to get prayer going for me and my family, prayer to protect my mind against Satan and get back to what God wanted me to do. The following morning I knew without a doubt that I was to start writing again. I had doubted this book so much over the past five years and now I knew with absolute certainty that I had to finish it. I then sent out emails and messages to my faithful friends, asking for prayer. I have to tell you that I am blessed with very sincere genuine friends. I almost feel God has hand-picked the best of the crop just for me. My darling Pastor George Dennison sends me a weekly email of encouragement and verses to keep me strong by and my wonderful friend Tracey Bridger from that Sunday of asking has NEVER missed a single day of encouragement. Every single day I receive a verse from the Bible. She sends it to me in such a beautiful form. LETS DECLARE TODAY: 'God is on my side, therefore I cannot be defeated', Romans 8:37 and Psalm 91 and Philippians 4:13.

This is the type of message I received each and every day and am still receiving now. It is almost as though God has chosen her to keep me strong and going each day. My other Ann seems to have been chosen to give me messages from God and seems to be the one that is going to be responsible for the publishing of this book through sources known to her. I must say that When I took time to sit and think about this book I sometimes got scared. There is so much involved in writing a book, more than one realizes. I started panicking one evening and then thought, 'Hey, what are you doing, you crazy woman? If this is from God, then He will provide every single thing you need. All He is asking me to do is to type.' So when I was writing and caught myself starting to panic, I said, 'Hey! God is in control here.'

I have received three strong messages in total from Ann. The first came on 9 March 2013. Ann said that God had awakened her and this is what He wanted her to tell me: 'Pauline, my child. I have heard your heart cry, and see you have done well, my child. You have dived into the deep end and thrown yourself at My feet. You have chosen Me above your family and I am going to open a door that *we* are going to walk through, and I will work through you. Continue to seek Me, and I am going to bless you.' She said that was the message and she felt the Lord's anointing as she wrote this. She also laughed and said, 'I'm sure He will let me go back to sleep now.'

The second message I received was on 20 February 2014: 'Pauline, last night I had a dream. This morning the Lord laid it on my heart to tell you *not* to be concerned. You are on His heart. I saw your mother and you in my dream. Your mother looked so much younger with natural brown hair, fatter and happy. In the dream she was *with* you in the decision you had to make, and she agreed with you. Then I heard the words: 'Pauline, don't be anxious. Your roots (UK Descendants) are going to help you and you will be supported from your "root". Pauline, today I read Matthew 28:20: "I am with you always, to the very end of the age." I have no idea what this all means but I do know that I have to send [the message] to you. I think it means that you are ready and that is why your mother agrees with you. He has chosen you to bless Him, it is coming and it will be a hard road to walk but you will be equipped.'

The third message I have told you but will add it in here. Received on 11 April 2015: 'Pauline. You are being equipped for a walk that the Lord is going to ask you to take with Him. Be ready for a change. You are in my prayers. Blessings.'

When it came to where I should publish my book, the minute I re-read message two I knew it was to be in the UK.

16

Changing

There is so much I can say about myself to you. I have spent most of my life as a confused, hurt and damaged person, always on my own, fighting the world. It feels as if I have been battling personal demons all my life. One of my biggest problems has been my weight. I have always had a fuller figure, and now I am in my fifties, you would think that I should have accepted that I am me and that's that. I love food, but from all my yo-yo dieting I have messed myself up completely. I don't think there is a diet I haven't tried. I used to starve myself when I first met ASJ. I wanted to be rake-thin for him. I went from being on the verge of anorexia to bulimia, and have suffered this disease most of my adult life. I think there are a lot of us with this disease but we are just too frightened to talk about it.

In the past I tried hypnotherapy; everything that a person can try, I have tried. Now I pray every day for God to fill me with the strength to overcome my weaknesses. I started dieting this year, January 2015, as I have put on so much weight. When my thyroid stopped working properly I just ate anything I wanted. Then I decided, 'Enough of this now!' I have lost weight, and so far I seem to be in control, though the devil may start attacking me in the area of my eating again.

I, as with you, have to deal with my weaknesses on a daily basis. I have not reached the stage yet as I did with smoking where the problem was just gone. I find certain issues have to just be dealt with daily. I pray every day for wisdom and discernment and patience and love and strength and peace. I also pray daily for forgiveness as I mess up so badly!

Jesus says, '… do not worry about tomorrow, for tomorrow will worry about itself' (Matthew 6:34).

He tells us to stop worrying ahead of ourselves. This is not always easy as I am a planner. I find being a disciple of Jesus is not easy. Some days I don't pray and I don't read my Bible or devotional books, and these are the days that I find I struggle with. One day can lead into two and into three and then all sorts of temptation comes and I just seem to give in and go with it. So I am trying very hard to discipline myself, which is not easy at all. Every day I keep on keeping on, and when I fail I get up and start again.

I seem to have spent most of my life on one form of a guilt trip or another. Guilt trips rob us of so much energy that could be spent on good thinking. I constantly try telling myself reasons why I should not feel guilt, but this is also an ongoing healing that will not find a solution overnight. Every day is a new day. New battles. New problems. But God gives us exactly what we need for each day. Jesus said that the most important commandment was to 'Love the Lord your God with all your heart and with all your soul and with all your mind and with all your strength' (Mark 12:30). I have four amazing children and I love them so deeply, so unconditionally, how can I love God more than them? I spent many years at war with this command until one day I said out loud, 'OK, Father God, You say I have to love You more than the precious gifts You have blessed me with. Teach me. Show me how to love You more. I am a mother and my instinct is to love and protect my children with my life. You say I have to love You first, then I say to You, teach me to love You first.' I have never battled this again! I love Jesus Christ with all my might and with all my soul and with all my strength, but I also love my children powerfully. I am human and I battle with many things, but am learning to take my problems to Jesus and get Him to help me to deal with everything. So much better than trying to do it in my strength!

God is always teaching me new things. I have this strange thing that I do quite often. When I am trying to make people feel comfortable, I sometimes make myself out to be very stupid. I am not quite sure why I think this will make the person I am with feel better, but they do seem to relax. Because I battled so much in the beginning with my Bible and not knowing where to find anything, I am inclined to do this with new people in church. I can see how they battle, and to make them feel at ease I tell them how useless I am with my Bible. But one day I was having tea with my friend Bev Dingle, and she looked at me and asked me why I do this. She had picked it up, but not many people do. Bev said to me that I am actually wrong in doing this as Jesus would not want me to allow people to think that I am stupid.

I find so many non-Christians are quick to point fingers at religious people and say, 'Did you see what so-and-so did? Well, I am so glad I am not a Christian.' I used to say this too until I gave my life to Jesus. But this poem sums up perfectly how I feel today:

WHEN I SAY, "I AM A CHRISTIAN"

When I say, "I am a Christian"
I'm not shouting, "I've been saved!"
I'm whispering, "I get lost sometimes
That's why I chose this way"

When I say, "I am a Christian"
I don't speak with human pride
I'm confessing that I stumble
Needing God to be my guide

When I say, "I am a Christian"
I'm not trying to be strong
I'm professing that I'm weak
And pray for strength to carry on

When I say, "I am a Christian"
I'm not bragging of success
I'm admitting that I've failed
And cannot ever pay the debt

When I say, "I am a Christian"
I don't think I know it all
I submit to my confusion
Asking humbly to be taught

Changing

When I say, "I am a Christian"
I'm not claiming to be perfect
My flaws are all too visible
But God believes I'm worth it

When I say, "I am a Christian"
I still feel the sting of pain
I have my share of heartache
That's why I seek God's name

When I say, "I am a Christian"
I do not wish to judge
I have no authority
I only know I'm loved

We are all broken and damaged somehow. I suppose there are some people out there who have somehow missed pain, but for the majority of ordinary people, we have all been in some form of pain and suffering at some stage of our lives, some far more than others. I have given up trying to question God and just believe that He has a plan. The problem I sometimes have is with His timing. His timing is not like our timing. This is where much prayer for patience comes in. I like everything done straight away! One way that God has taught me patience is through life as a carer.

I still do things that are not right, but honestly do try to do good. I have a rule that I never ever look at a married man, even if he is gorgeous and convincing. This is an area, I am sad to say, where I have almost failed... twice. I have managed to walk away before any damage was done, but I so easily get caught in that trap of receiving attention. But I am changing, slowly, with God's help. I was a scared woman but I am now bolder and braver. I am able to walk into places on my own. If I get nervous I have learnt how to speak very confidently without giving any clue as to my inner feelings. I keep looking to Jesus!

I am always bringing my requests to Jesus in prayer. Most times when I pray for really important things or I need an answer to a problem or a decision needs to be made, God often makes me wait until the last minute. This is torture, but I hang in there, pleading most of the time for Him to answer me! He often makes me wait. Do you find this, too? I am sure this is how He builds trust and faith in us. Mike Kruger used to always tell me that Jesus will always answer us. He called it the four Ds: Direct, Delay, Denial, Different. Yes, He will always answer, and we need to be aware of His answer. It is not always what we want, as He can see the big picture that we cannot see, and He knows what is best for us.

My values in life have changed. I have a great sense of hope now. Peace is a gift that God offers us through Jesus. Having God's peace does not mean we won't have problems or sorrow in this life. The Lord does not want us to worry or lose hope, and that is why He promises us His peace. If we ask for peace, He will grant it to us. 'Peace I leave with you; my peace I give you. I do not give to you as the world gives. Do not let your hearts be troubled and do not be afraid' (John 14:27).

I found that when I gave my life to Jesus, I discovered a freedom, and a new pattern of life began, very slowly and without me even noticing, but it was definitely there. I need Jesus and I need His peace to help me get through each day. I still catch myself trying to do life in my own strength and sadly fall flat on my face. When I start becoming very anxious about certain things, I have learnt to take deep breaths and just call on Jesus over and over until I feel calm.

Jesus invites us so clearly when He says, 'Come to me, all you who are weary and burdened, and I will give you rest' (Matthew 11:28), and yet we just carry on trying our own solutions instead of just accepting His invitation and seeing what it will bring. I have suffered so much depression in my life. When I'm depressed, everything feels so dark and I have no hope and feel so sorry for myself, but I have learnt to fight this. Light is much stronger than dark, and even though all I want to do is be left alone to wallow in my self-pity, I fight back now. I force myself to read my Bible and to draw hope and comfort from the knowledge that Jesus loves me and cares about me. Satan wants me to feel fear, loneliness, anguish, self-pity, worthlessness, but the light brings relief and safety and hope and peace. As long as I have Jesus I will fight darkness. He is my comforter, my redeemer, my healer, my provider, my protector, my friend, my shepherd, my peace-giver; God is my *abba* Father. Depression wants to rob us of life and happiness.

I asked God daily for over a year to please give me my home. I then changed my plea to thanksgiving. I started thanking Him for giving me my home. Then one day my son said to me, 'Don't you think you expect too much from

God?' I was quite shocked that he didn't see things the way I saw them. Everything I have is from God. I ask Him for a lot of different things; sometimes He gives them to me and other times I keep hearing in my mind, 'Pauline, My grace is sufficient for you, my girl!' (see 2 Corinthians 12:9) and then I know I'm not going to get what I have been asking for. This, by the way, is not what I want to hear, and I do often put up a good argument as to all the reasons why I believe I do deserve it! I am only human. I strive to be more like Jesus, but know I will never get there in this lifetime... still, I am changing. *He* is changing me.

17

My Ongoing Walk

MY BIBLE = BASIC INSTRUCTIONS BEFORE LEAVING EARTH

This, by the way, was taught to me by a six-year-old. I kid you not. This should give you an idea of how much I knew about my Bible. Absolutely nothing and trust me, I still know very little about the Bible, really, but I keep reading and learning. I pray for a deep hunger to want to read my Bible more than I do. I listen to some people who can quote verses out of the Bible and think, 'I wish I was like that!'

As you may know, the Bible is divided into two sections. The first is about everything that happened before the Son of God, Jesus, came to earth, and the second is about His life here, and what happened after He died.

I used to find the Old Testament confusing until I started going to Bible studies and reading my Bible more. As with anything, the more you study it the better you get at it. I am never going to understand my Bible completely, but I do believe that Jesus has not finished teaching me yet. This is why I believe Bible studies and church are so important. We need to keep feeding ourselves in order to grow. I hear people saying, 'I don't have to go to church to be a Christian!' Whilst this may be true, how much growth can we achieve on our own? Half the time I have no idea what I am reading, and need to go to people who have more knowledge than me, so I can learn from them. We need to grow in order to allow our light to shine; I want people to know what God has done for me, that I have been forgiven, and that I love Jesus Christ very much.

My current pastor, Barry Wyatt, once gave an excellent illustration of why we should go to church. He said, 'Look into a huge fire and watch it burn down until we have only coals left. Take one of those coals out of the fire and put it aside and watch how quickly it cools down till it's cold. Look back at the fire, and you will see the amber of the coals all together still glowing.' The Bible itself tells us we should keep meeting together (see Hebrews 10:24-25). When dark clouds enter our lives it is so much easier to sit and wallow in our own problems, but when this happens to me, I force myself to go to church and keep faithful to God.

There is no shame in not understanding your Bible. If you are new to it, and are going to a really good Bible study group, the person leading should pick up quickly that you are struggling and hopefully will very discreetly help you along. Please don't do what I did the first time I went to a Bible study, and run away! Pray for boldness to stay. Pray for a friend to sit with you who will help you. As you attend more Bible studies, you will slowly start to understand your Bible more and more.

Trust me, I still have a mountain of stuff to learn. One thing that is far too big for my mind is the Trinity. How on earth can one plus one plus one equal one? But it does! God the Father and God the the Son and God the Holy Spirit are three in one... yes, three, yet one.

I have had people trying to make me doubt my Bible. I just believe it for what it is. If Jesus said it, then that's it. I have far too many faults to still have doubting my Bible as one of them! I love the promises in the Bible, and it is so full of them. I often write one down and then will cheekily keep reminding Jesus that He never ever breaks a promise. Another thing I do that is naughty is this – if someone does something nasty to me, I walk away and look up and say, 'Did You see that, Father? Did You?' I almost feel better knowing that Jesus has acknowledged how I was treated... but then, I need to remember how *I* treat people!

One of my favourite sayings is this:

DON'T CURSE IT
DON'T NURSE IT
DON'T REHEARSE IT
DISPERSE IT AND WATCH GOD REVERSE IT

I love this. If someone is nasty to us an immediate reaction is to get nasty back. Remembering this saying is how I manage to control this emotion. I don't always succeed, but as I said earlier, I am a work in progress.

I want to share with you some of my favourite promises from the Bible. I love to read my Bible and then say, 'OK, this promise is the one I choose for today.' Some of my favourites are:

'I will never leave you nor forsake you (Joshua 1:5).

'For I am the LORD your God who takes hold of your right hand and says to you, Do not fear; I will help you' (Isaiah 41:13).

'Do not be afraid, for I am with you' (Isaiah 43:5).

'For I know the plans I have for you,' declares the LORD, 'plans to prosper you and not to harm you, plans to give you hope and a future' (Jeremiah 29:11).

'So if the Son sets you free, you will be free indeed' (John 8:36).

'And even the very hairs of your head are all numbered. So don't be afraid' (Matthew 10:30-31).

I love the promises that God gives us about never leaving us or forsaking us or abandoning us. If God says it, then I believe it. See Deuteronomy 31:6 and 31:8, 1 Kings 8:57, 1 Chronicles 28:20, Psalms 37:28 and 94:14, Isaiah 41:17 and 42:16, and Hebrews 13:5.

I read the Psalms often, as I find they relate to my life on a daily basis. The Psalms showcase prayers, praise and complaints to God. Over the years, whilst going through very difficult times, I have found that reciting the first four verses of Psalm 23 has helped me cope with some terrible situations. It has almost given me air to breathe:

The LORD is my shepherd, I lack nothing.
He makes me lie down in green pastures,
he leads me beside quiet waters,
he refreshes my soul.

He guides me along the right paths
for his name's sake.
Even though I walk
through the darkest valley,
I will fear no evil,
for you are with me;
your rod and your staff,
they comfort me.

The more I said it, the more I understood the power in these four verses. I have walked out of much heartache with these comforting words.

In January 2012, my late mother's best friend, Pat van Eek, sent me this message, typed out, and I have clung to these words all these years. It is from the Good News Translation, and the text is Isaiah 43:18-19:

Do not cling to events of the past
or dwell on what happened long ago.
Watch for the new thing I am going to do.
It is happening already – you can see it now!
I will make a road through the wilderness
and give you streams of water there.

I believe that my heavenly Father is going to bring new things into my life, but it will happen in His time and not mine. This promise is not only intended for me but also for you. How great is that!

I find that if I do not have my personal time with God in the morning – my 'quiet time' – my day will be a struggle. I definitely have better days when I start my day with Jesus.

As well as reading my devotions and my Bible, I love to write down what I'm asking for, or who I am praying for, or a wonderful promise that I just read. I keep a journal, and whatever is on my heart is what Jesus gets bombarded with. I talk to God as I would have spoken to my human father.

In the year 2007 I was invited to go on the Emmaus Walk. I had absolutely no idea what it was about, except I was told that I was not allowed a phone or a watch. It was at the time in Stutterheim in South Africa, and was taking place from a Thursday to the Sunday. I was taken along and dropped off, and felt really scared and nervous as I never knew a soul there. I stood against a wall and looked at the many faces of the women there.

A woman caught my eye as she paced up and down, and I just knew that I was going to approach her to try to make friends with her. Her name was Judy Codner, and she now lives in the UK – I mentioned her earlier, when I said I only knew one person in Britain when I first arrived! The second woman I was drawn to was called Tammy Kelly. This woman has been a faithful friend, handpicked for me by God. The third woman I made friends with was Donnae Thomas. She is another 'rock' given to me by Jesus. These three ladies have seen me through many a bad time.

The Emmaus Walk was wonderful, reading the Bible and finding out more about Jesus and His plans for us. The idea of the walk is based in the story found in chapter 24 of Luke's Gospel about the disciples who met the Lord on the road to a place called Emmaus. This was after He had been crucified and had risen from the dead. They did not recognize Him, but were discussing all the things that had happened, and He explained things to them as they walked along. They eventually realized who He was as He shared a meal with them.

As we shared life together on that three-day walk, we experienced how much Jesus loves us and wants us to be obedient servants.

Conclusion

Let me tell you something. Airing one's own dirty laundry for everyone to read is not easy, but this is what Jesus has told me to do. I am a very private person in many ways, but I have been told to go out and tell whoever is interested to read my life's secrets. It hasn't been easy, but this is where faithfulness comes in. If this is what it takes to help just one person come to Jesus, then it is worth it.

Perhaps you do not know Jesus. Maybe you have read my book and seen that I am just an ordinary woman, a woman with struggles, who has an extraordinary God. So now I say to you, would you like to join me in this walk with Jesus?

Jesus does not promise you a rose garden, but He does promise peace and joy, a filling of the Holy Spirit. He can promise you that you will never be alone again. He can promise you that you will begin to change. Maybe you won't even notice some of the changes that will take place in you, they will be so very gradual. Jesus can promise you a relationship like nothing you have ever experienced before. Jesus Christ is mighty and powerful and huge and loving and caring and wants you so badly so that He can show you what living is all about.

I gave my life to Jesus in the year 2000 and have never ever regretted my decision. With all the hardships that I have gone through and am going through, just knowing that Jesus loves me unconditionally and will never leave me nor forsake me is enough to keep me going. I still do things that I know are wrong, but with God's help, as I surrender to His Son, I am aiming to be the perfect little girl for Jesus. I often remind Him I am His little girl. Even though I fall on a regular basis I have meaning to stand up again. Jesus puts His hand out to us and all we have to do is take it.

In this book I have mentioned the work that Jesus did on the cross in order to save us. We were sinners, enemies of God, but God loved us so much He sent His Son to pay the price we could never pay so we could be right with Him, live in fellowship with Him today, and be with Him for all eternity. This is something we cannot do ourselves. We cannot make ourselves clean. Jesus does it for us. The sinner's prayer is a prayer of repentance. It is repenting of sins committed, and expresses a desire to have a personal relationship with the living God.

Are you ready to change your life? Do you want God to take over? If you are ready to start your journey in life, repeat this prayer:

Father God, I need You. I admit I am a sinner. Please forgive me. Thank You, Jesus, for dying on the cross for my sins. I believe You rose again from the dead, and I now open the door of my life and receive You as my Lord and

Saviour. Thank You for forgiving my sins and for giving me eternal life. I ask You now, Father, to take control of my life and to make me the person You want me to be. Please come into my heart and my life and teach me to trust and follow You. Thank You, Father. Praise You, Father. Bless You, Father. Amen.

I would advise you to find a church near to you, or one where you feel comfortable and welcome, and tell the pastor or church leader of the commitment you have just made. Do not leave it too long as the Bible says it is important that you tell someone what you have done (see Romans 10:9-10). The sooner you can get prayer going for you the better. As a brand-new Christian you will need support from a church. If you are like me and afraid to go on your own, then ask Jesus to send someone to you to help you to overcome this barrier. Please don't just leave it; you could ring your local church and tell them that you would like to come. They will hopefully then meet you on the door. Ask God to lead you to the church He wants you to worship Him in, a Bible-believing, Spirit-filled church where you can learn about this wonderful God we serve. I never even asked God what church I should go to; He led me without me even knowing it. The power of our God!

Probably the easiest thing we can do is give our lives to Jesus. There are no exams to write or forms to fill in, or permission to be obtained from other people. It is so simple; maybe *too* simple, and that is why we doubt and stall in doing this. Once we have come to Him, our lives will begin to change. These are the steps to your personal revival:

1. Repent of every known sin. (see Joel 2:12-13; 2 Corinthians 7:9-10; James 4:4-10; Revelation 2:5)
2. Forsake all questionable habits and activities. (see Romans 13:14; Romans 14:14; 1 Corinthians 10:31; Galatians 5:19-21)
3. Make right any wrongs between yourself and others. (see Matthew 6:14-15; Matthew 18:15-35; Romans 12:17-21; Colossians 3:12-15)
4. Communicate with God through prayer and the Bible. (see Psalm 119:107b; Mark 11:22-26; John 16:23-24; John 17:17; Colossians 3:15-16; 1 Thessalonians 5:17; 1 John 2:1-3)
5. Trust God to use you as His instrument in the lives of others. (John 15:16, Ephesians 2:10, Colossians 4:5-6, 2 Timothy 2:20-21, James 5:19-20 and Jude 22-23)

Another step in discipleship is baptism in water. When we decide to follow Christ, we die to ourselves and are raised to new life in Him, and water baptism illustrates this. When I eventually got baptized I was on a high for days afterwards! When you are ready for this step in your life Jesus will start convicting you by His Holy Spirit, who comes to live in us when we are born again – that is, when we ask Jesus to be our Lord and Saviour. Jesus gives us His Spirit so we can live for Him.

To be a Christian is not a one-off thing, it is a daily walk with Jesus. Remember that at first it is all just baby steps. Do not try to run before you have learnt to crawl. I have seen brand-new Christians rush ahead and burn out before they even really get started. Keep in step with Jesus. He will lead you and guide you and show you. He will send the people you need in your life for your walk with Him. Trust Him.

Another thing I wanted to say to you that genuinely works for me is when you catch yourself worrying about this and that, try to do the following.

1. Write down each and every worry that you have.
2. Calmly pray about each one of these worries.
3. Prayerfully confirm that God is in full control of every situation, and that worry will no longer affect your tranquillity and peace of mind.

Another thing I do when I catch myself worrying or starting to panic about something is this: I simply look up and quietly say, 'Jesus, I need you.' The secret is to take our burdens to God in prayer. If you do this you will soon start to discover that Jesus is in fact all-sufficient; He is all you need, today, tomorrow, and always. So just walk away and leave the problem, ugliness, whatever it may be, in the hands of Jesus, as He will see to it.

Also, very, very important – give thanks every day to Jesus. Praise Him and Thank Him daily. I sat one day and started saying, 'Thank You' for all I had and eventually gave up as the thank yous just went on and on and on. I want to try to count my blessings instead of all the negatives.

The way I see it, you have absolutely nothing to lose by making this commitment and watching the changes that come into your life. Make time in the morning for a 'quiet time' with God. Read a psalm and say a prayer for yourself and for others. As I said earlier, I have found that on the days that I have not done this, I have really battled.

I want my life to glorify Jesus. I want to say that you are not the only one going through a tough time. We are not alone with our problems. Jesus is waiting for you. He is only a prayer away.

God does not lie. God does not go back on His word like people do. He speaks to us in different ways. Either through His Word, the Bible, or quietly in our hearts, or through someone else. If God wants to tell us something, He will make us understand.

Sometimes He speaks directly to us. About a year and a half ago I woke up and clearly heard God telling me that a certain person was hungry. I kept thinking I knew no such person, and turned over and went back to sleep. Five times I was woken up and told to feed this person as she was hungry. I eventually said, 'OK! I will try to find this person.' I started quietly asking around the church if we had a person by this name and was shocked to find out that we did and she was really battling. Was this truly God who had spoken to me? If it wasn't, then who else could it be? 'Yes, Lord,' I said. 'Your will be done!' I immediately arranged meals to be delivered to her daily and sent an envelope with some money to her monthly. When God wants something done, He will provide what is needed. Whether it be money, or wisdom, or knowledge, or whatever, You will be equipped to do whatever He asks.

Working for God is unbelievably fulfilling. He might just ask you to pray for someone; sometimes you will be busy and suddenly a face just pops into your mind… well, I believe that is the Holy Spirit asking us to pray. Just doing that makes you feel so special and needed.

God takes natural people to do His supernatural work. We were not all born to stand out as important people for God; He needs the 'little people' too. He needs us to help other people who are battling in life. Just praying sincerely for someone in need is a big deal to God. Nobody sees it except God, but He is the only one who really counts. It is a big deal to me that God sees what I do for Him. Not people, but God. It is Him I am out to please. This, I must add, is very difficult and I fail Him daily with sin, yet He picks me up and dusts me off and we start all over again because He loves me. He loves you in the same way. You are not reading this book by accident. You are doing exactly what God wants you to do.

The following verses from the Bible prove how much God loves us:

'I took you from the ends of the earth, from its farthest corners I called you. I said, "You are my servant"; I have chosen you and have not rejected you' (Isaiah 41:9).

'Before I formed you in the womb I knew you, before you were born I set you apart; I appointed you as a prophet to the nations' (Jeremiah 1:5).

'For he chose us in him before the creation of the world to be holy and blameless in his sight' (Ephesians 1:4).

'And we know that in all things God works for the good of those who love him, who have been called according to His purpose' (Romans 8:28).

'Who will bring any charge against those whom God has chosen? It is God who justifies. Who then is the one who condemns? No one. Christ Jesus who died – more than that, who was raised to life – is at the right hand of God and is also interceding for us' (Romans 8:33-34).

Read these promises from God carefully.

When we read verses such as the ones above, we may find some people will tell us that God is not speaking to us, but to the people of that time. But the Holy Spirit convicts and instructs us through the Scriptures. Satan works through people and, sadly, many times through the ones we love the most. Satan does not want us to increase in faith or trust in God, so we will experience attacks. If and when this happens, never forget that the God we serve is way more powerful. Why do we believe these lies? I spent almost my entire life believing that I was worth nothing. I have believed every lie Satan has ever told me. Why? Why do we allow this? Is it not time to take a stand against him?

When I look at the big picture, everything seems to fit together. I am always busy, always on the go, so much to do and so little time to do it. People that know me will tell you this is me through and through. I keep praying every day, 'Lord, my Father, my *abba*, my daddy, please reveal Your purpose for my life. Father, what is it You want me to do to glorify Your name? What, Father? Please show me, Father.' So here I am writing a book! I want to tell you that I have never written a thing in my life. What do I know about writing? But I cannot believe that this is not part of God's big plan for my life.

I have prayed for so long that my life would really belong to God. I have asked Him for so long to mould me into what He wants me to be. Although I have so many faults, I say to you: 'God loves us despite all this.' You are not reading this book by accident or by a coincidence; this is what God is trying to tell you, the same as He tried for years and years to tell me. I don't believe we read certain books by accident. I believe that the Holy Spirit guides us to try to open our eyes to the greatness of the wonderful God we serve. He loves you regardless of all your sin, evil-doing, hardships, trials.

We all face hardships and trials in life, but how would we grow in Him if we didn't suffer? Every time I have been down, flat on my face, I have always turned to God for help. We live in the world, and we trust the world more than we trust God. We need to turn this around and trust God first and then watch what happens in our lives.

You can see by what I have written in this book that God is a forgiving God, a loving God, and a God who never gives up on us. Why does He bother with us? Simply because He loves us and wants us to turn from our old ways, to Him. When we live without God in the world, we may think we are happy but still feel empty. When we live with the Lord, we feel a peace that only God can give us. So even when life gets difficult, and it will, we have what only people who live with God have – His peace. This is what makes dealing with problems easier. No matter how difficult the situation, God will make a way for us. God is way bigger than our problems, and He loves us; He wants good things for us.

Just after I lost my job, I read a book about George Müller. I had never heard of him before. I was blown away by this man's faith in God. As a boy he stole money, as a young man he was a swindler, and as an adult he found God – and God trusted him with a fortune. He kept very little for himself. He was not driven by pride or greed, but was humble and realized that all the money he was given was not his but God's. He never asked a single person for a thing, only relied on God. He lived in the nineteenth century, and ran orphanages, Sunday schools, regular schools, distributed Bibles and supported missionaries. He did all this through the grace of God.

I read in his book that one day all the orphans sat down to lunch and the helpers were very worried as there was not a scrap of food to feed the children. George Müller said to them that they should thank God for the food they were about to receive, when a knock came at the door – a baker had baked three batches of bread for the orphans; then a milk cart broke down outside, and so there was enough milk for all the children.

What God did for George Müller, He can do for us. Believe Him, have faith in Him, and trust Him. George Müller never asked anyone for a thing; he only ever asked God. That is what we have to do. This way of living is not easy, and we can only do this through lots of prayer and reading God's Word, and mixing with other Christians

It has taken me a long time to get my mind around this praying thing. Why is praying so important? Let me tell you. Praying is exactly the same as a conversation. You talk to God, and God talks to you. God wants us to talk to Him every day, as often as we want to. In Matthew 6:8 Jesus says, '… your Father knows what you need before you ask him.' So why must we ask, if God knows our need already? Because He wants to talk to us. He wants this conversation with us. This is why praying is so important. After we are finished asking God for our daily needs and praying for others, we should really just sit quietly in His company and wait on Him; we should also give thanks to Him and praise Him for all He does for us.

I want to tell you about the title of this book. God clearly kept telling me I had to use the word 'ordinary'. Over and over I came across this 'ordinary' word. I kept saying, 'Yes, Lord, I know I am ordinary. Why is this so important?' God kept saying that this book was for all the ordinary people out there; people that believe themselves to be not special at all. God wants ordinary people to do the extraordinary for Him! God is calling you to Himself. Be honest – how many times have you felt that secret, silent nudge? Your time is now. God waited thirty-seven years for me to turn to Him. How many years has He been waiting for you?

Every person who gives their lives to Jesus are given gifts. Every one of us have a different gift. One or maybe more are given to you by the Holy Spirit. Read Romans 12, 1 Corinthians 12, and Ephesians 4 and 1 John 4:1-11. Examples of these gifts are: prophecy, healing, teaching, serving, speaking in tongues – that is, other languages that God gives us that we have not learnt.

We have to keep reminding ourselves that these gifts are given to glorify our God. They are also given to lift up other believers. We must use our gifts to serve others. If we are given a gift that puts us in the limelight, such as healing, we must remember to constantly tell people it is not done in our strength but in God's. We must be very careful not to adopt an attitude of pride. We are nothing without God. We must constantly pray for humility. No gift given from God is less important than another. There is no rank.

Next I must share with you about the fruit of the Spirit. This is different to the spiritual gifts. We read in Galatians 5:22-23 of the nine fruits of the Holy Spirit. These are: 'love, joy, peace, forbearance, kindness, goodness, faithfulness, gentleness and self-control'. These began to come so quietly into my life that I never noticed them until my daughter pointed out the change in me. They sneak in and change us slowly, for the better.

Let me tell you from personal experience that this is only the start of life with Jesus. As I expect you have seen from my story, when you become a Christian your problems don't just go away! Satan is going to do everything in his power to stop you getting close to Christ. Are you ready to fight? Never forget you are no longer on your own, God fights for you. Satan doesn't worry about you when you aren't a Christian because you are where he wants you, but if you are about to step out for Jesus he will keep trying to get you back.

My life *will* glorify Jesus. People will come to see that even the worst sinners are loved by Jesus. I am not a preacher or a theologian, I am just an ordinary person, glorifying God's name with my life. If you met me today and knew me ten years ago, you would never believe this is the same person. In the past I needed substances to give me courage; now I have Jesus. I can walk into any room on my own. I can talk up boldly – sometimes I even shock myself. The Holy Spirit has changed me in a very big way. I still get scared but now I have Jesus with me, helping me.

I am broken, I am damaged, but I am standing and I am healing.

I truly pray that you will join me on my journey with Jesus, and find what you have been searching for your entire life.

Contact Details

You can contact me by email:
pauline.autobiography@gmail.com

or on my Facebook page:
Ordinary People Finding Jesus